A HORRID HISTORY

OF CHRISTMAS

HORRIBLE HAPPENINGS &
FRIGHTENING FESTIVITIES

NICOLA SLY

First published 2012

The History Press
The Mill, Brimscombe Port
Stroud, Gloucestershire, GL5 2QG
www.thehistorypress.co.uk

British Library Cataloguing in Publication Data.
A catalogue record for this book is available from the British Library.

ISBN 978 0 7524 7645 2

Typesetting and origination by The History Press
Printed in India

CONTENTS

INTRODUCTION
& ACKNOWLEDGEMENTS

CHRISTMAS IS USUALLY thought of as a happy time but, to quote *The Times* of 26 December 1910, 'It is curious how Christmastide has been associated with disasters of all kinds'. The paper then goes on to list some of these Christmas disasters, beginning with no less than sixteen rail accidents occurring in the United Kingdom between 1864 and 1906, which collectively resulted in almost 200 fatalities. Yet, if rail travel during the festive season seems dangerous, there are other activities which are equally perilous, such as playing football, shooting, working, ice skating, visiting relatives, going to parties or pantomimes, eating and, perhaps deadliest of all, the consumption of copious quantities of alcohol.

The following gruesome collection of true tales of Christmas past, drawn entirely from accounts in the contemporary newspapers listed in the bibliography at the rear of the book, serves to illustrate that the festive season is not always associated with peace on earth and goodwill to all men. However, much as today, not everything in the historical newspapers was reported accurately and there were frequent discrepancies between publications, with differing dates and variations in names and spelling.

As always, I must thank my editor at The History Press, Matilda Richards, for seeing this book through from the initial idea to

Skating on the Serpentine could be a dangerous pastime. (Author's collection)

print and, on a more personal level, my husband Richard for his love and support.

Every effort has been made to clear copyright, however, my apologies to anyone I may have inadvertently missed. I can assure you it was not deliberate but an oversight on my part.

Finally, wherever and whenever you're reading this, I would like to wish every one of my readers a very happy Christmas and hope that your future festive celebrations are always calamity and catastrophe free.

Nicola Sly, 2012

SOUTH WEST

Devonport, Plymouth

On Christmas Eve 1885, twenty-year-old Ella Mary Fitzroy and her eighteen-year-old sister Maud of Plymouth, Devon were getting ready to go to a ball when Ella's dress accidentally came into contact with a lighted candle and, within seconds, she was enveloped in a ball of flames.

She rushed screaming from her bedroom onto the landing. Maud ran to help her sister and tried to beat out the flames, but her own dress caught fire and she fled downstairs in a state of panic. Her stepfather, Edward St Aubyn, wrapped her in a blanket but both girls were extensively burned.

Surgeon Mr Toms attended and found that both girls were burned all over their bodies. He administered morphine to ease their excruciating pain but Maud succumbed on Christmas Day, while Ella lingered until 11 January 1886. Inquests later returned verdicts of accidental death on both girls.

Winchcomb

Towards the end of 1864, fifty-year-old retired surgeon Richard Smith of Winchcomb, Gloucestershire began to behave in a most peculiar manner. He became convinced that he was about to be kidnapped and sent to America and was sometimes seen sitting at the side of the road, 'fishing' with a rod and line.

On 27 December, the Smiths' sons visited their parents and saw nothing unusual about their father's behaviour, although when they left, their father cautioned them to run all the way home as he feared they would be waylaid and robbed. At nine o'clock, a neighbour heard what sounded like a gunshot coming from Smith's house. She went outside and listened but could only hear Smith talking and the sound of furniture being moved.

The next morning, a woman called on the Smiths to buy milk. Richard Smith seemed perfectly normal, although he made no reply when the woman asked how his wife was. Soon afterwards, Smith's sons were at their work on a farm when they saw their father walking towards them.

'Where's your sister?' Smith asked them conversationally and, when told that Martha was not there, he continued casually, 'Your mother's dead.'

The young men were so shocked that they struggled to comprehend their father's words, although they deduced from his rambling explanation that he had had a gun in his hand, which went off accidentally, killing his wife. One boy went for the police, while the other went to his parents' cottage, finding Sarah Smith lying dead on the floor in the parlour.

Smith was charged with wilful murder and appeared at the Gloucester Assizes in April 1865. The current Winchcomb surgeon believed that he had been mentally unsound for at least twenty years and it was obvious to all concerned that Smith was not in his right mind. Having heard the details of the case, the jury needed only five minutes to find him guilty but insane and he was ordered to be confined as a criminal lunatic for the rest of his life.

Bristol

At about five o'clock in the afternoon of Christmas Day 1850, the Wooles family of The Blue Bowl Tavern in Tottersdown, Bristol, were preparing tea when a petty argument about toast sprang up between them. After a piece of toast was burned, Samuel Wooles threw it onto the fire and decreed that nobody would have toast that afternoon. His wife, Hannah (or Harriet) retaliated, telling Samuel that if she wanted toast she would have it, and went to another room to get some more bread. Samuel followed her and slapped his wife hard across the face.

The couple's youngest son, Thomas, asked his father what he did that for and Samuel picked up a stick and swung it at the young man. Thomas seized the first thing that came to hand with which to defend himself, which happened to be a gun that his older brother had carelessly left lying around. Although Thomas didn't aim the gun at his father or pull the trigger, it went off and Samuel was shot in the groin.

Hearing the gunshot, a neighbour rushed in and found Samuel lying on a settle moaning, 'I shall die, I shall die.' Thomas was horrified by what had just happened, begging the neighbour to run for a surgeon and repeating again and again, 'I didn't know the gun was loaded.'

When surgeon Robert Ellis arrived, Samuel had been put to bed. Ellis found a large round hole in Wooles's abdomen and quickly realised that Wooles was mortally wounded. He died at about nine o'clock that evening.

At an inquest held by coroner Mr R. Uphill, the dead man's oldest son, who was also called Samuel, explained that he bought his gun downstairs on Christmas morning in the hope of shooting a pigeon. By the time he got downstairs, the pigeons had flown away, so Samuel junior put his gun to one side and promptly forgot all about it. The inquest jury learned that there was no quarrel between father and son and that when Wooles learned that there was no hope for him, he asked to see a solicitor to make a will, leaving his fortune to be divided equally between Samuel and Thomas. This act alone suggested that the shooting was not deliberate, theorised the coroner, since Wooles obviously bore no malice towards his youngest son.

The inquest jury accepted the coroner's suggestion that this was a parricide by misadventure rather than a deliberate act of violence, returning a verdict that the deceased was 'accidentally shot'.

Taunton

On Boxing Day 1882, Anna 'Nance' Roswell was enjoying a quiet drink with friends in the Crown and Tower Inn in Silver Street, Taunton, when Frederick Ripley entered the pub and said, 'Nance, I want to speak with you.' The couple left the pub together and, minutes later, Nance staggered back, bleeding heavily from a single stab wound in her throat. A doctor was called and a cab summoned to take her to hospital, but she bled to death shortly after her arrival.

Nance and Ripley had been 'walking out' together for four years but Ripley was extremely jealous and Nance had ended their relationship as a result. Arrested and charged with her murder, Ripley told the police, 'I done it.'

Tried for murder at the Somerset Assizes before Mr Justice Baggallay, Ripley insisted that he had been drinking at the time and had never intended to hurt his former girlfriend. In a written statement, he told the court that he was destitute, mainly because he had spent all his money on clothes for Anna, including the jacket that she was wearing when she died. Believing that Anna had ended their relationship because he had no money, he asked her for the return of the jacket and, when she refused and slapped his face he tried to cut it off her, accidentally stabbing her in the throat as he did so.

Ripley's defence argued that he was insane, due to the effects of drink and that the offence was manslaughter rather than murder, on the grounds that Anna had provoked him by slapping him. However, the jury disagreed, finding twenty-one-year-old Ripley guilty of wilful murder, although recommending mercy on the grounds of his youth and previous good character. Although sentenced to death, Ripley was later reprieved and sent to Portland Prison in Dorset.

Portland Convict Prison. (Author's collection)

Note: In contemporary reports of the case, the victim's name is variously recorded as Ann, Annie or Anna Roswell, Rowsell and Russell.

Awliscombe

The Pring family of Awliscombe, Devon, were planning to spend Christmas Day 1852 at the farm in the village owned by Mr Pring senior. As twelve-year-old Ann waited to leave in the porch with her cousin Mary Haynes and the family servant, there was a sudden bang and Ann dropped to the ground dead.

Ann's father, Francis, had already left to go to his father's farm and, before doing so, had asked his wife's nephew, John Wall, to fire a few shots in a newly planted wheat field to scare away rooks. Francis Pring had left the gun in a bacon rack in the kitchen but he neglected to mention that it was loaded and, when John picked it up, he pulled the trigger, accidentally shooting his cousin Ann behind the ear.

It was in a way fortunate that Ann took the full force of the blast, since John was only 3 or 4 feet away when the gun was fired and could easily have killed Mary Haynes and the servant too. As it was, the other two women suffered only minor injuries. The fact that the inquest returned a verdict of 'accidental death' was of little comfort to Wall, who was said to be much distressed by the shooting.

Plymouth

In 1858, the 17th Foot Regiment and the 2nd Warwick Militia were both quartered in the Citadel in Plymouth and for many months there had been bad blood between them. On Boxing Day, the underlying tension boiled over when Sergeant Henry Clay of the Warwicks went into The George and Dragon public house in Stonehouse Lane.

A number of the 17th Regiment were already drinking there and one told Clay, 'There's none of your sort here.'

Clay took exception to the man's tone and ordered his men to draw their bayonets. The 17th Regiment saw this as a challenge and a physical fight broke out, during which the 17th Regiment lashed out at the Warwicks with their brass-tipped belts. Charles Lawler was in the act of striking Clay when Clay plunged his bayonet six inches into his opponent's chest. The point penetrated a large artery near Lawler's heart and he rushed back into the pub shouting 'I'm stabbed', dying from internal haemorrhage within five minutes.

An inquest returned a verdict of manslaughter against Clay, who was tried at the Devon Lent Assizes in March 1859. There were a number of witnesses, all giving conflicting evidence, but as the case progressed it began to appear more and more as if the 17th Regiment were the aggressors.

Twenty-two-year-old Clay was known as a mild, inoffensive man, who was an excellent soldier. Immediately after the stabbing, witnesses noted that he had marks of a blow on his face and it was pointed out that, if used with force, the belts wielded by the 17th Regiment could easily fracture a man's skull.

Clay's defence counsel insisted that their client had no intention of hurting anyone, but was defending himself against a brutal attack when Lawler accidentally ran onto his bayonet.

The trial judge summed up the evidence for the jury, stating that he personally believed that Clay was justified in giving an order to draw bayonets, since it was his duty to ensure the safety

Plymouth Citadel. (Author's collection)

of his own men. He asked the jury to decide if Clay deliberately struck the blow or if Lawler rushed onto the bayonet and the jury gave Clay the benefit of the doubt, finding him not guilty after a brief deliberation.

Bristol

Thirty-eight-year-old George Drewett, the former manager of a tannery in Bedminster, had taken a new job in Plymouth and returned to Bristol to arrange for his family to join him there but, on Christmas morning 1882, he was suddenly taken ill and died within hours. A post-mortem examination showed that he was suffering from acute meningitis.

On 5 March 1882, Drewett had tried to commit suicide by shooting himself in the head and the bullet was so deeply embedded in his brain that it was impossible to remove surgically. Even so, Drewett apparently made a complete recovery and showed no ill effects from the shooting. Charged with attempted suicide, he assured magistrates that he no longer had any wish to kill himself and was discharged.

Doctors thought it unlikely that the shooting was in any way connected to the meningitis that ultimately killed Drewett.

Broker's Wood, near Trowbridge

Early on the morning of Boxing Day 1896, Henry Turner walked into the police station at Westbury, Wiltshire and told officers there that he wished to give himself up for murdering his wife. Asked for more information, Turner explained that he and his wife had not quarrelled but he had simply hit her over the head with a hatchet earlier that morning then locked his house door and come to turn himself in.

The police officers rushed to Turner's cottage with a surgeon. Once inside, they could hear moaning coming from upstairs, where they found Sarah Jane Turner lying face-up on her bed, her head hanging over the edge. She died soon afterwards without regaining consciousness, at which point Turner was charged with her murder. 'I thought she'd be better dead than alive,' he explained, adding, 'if she died, she'd go to heaven'.

An inquest heard that sixty-year-old Turner was known as a sober, hard-working and steady man. However, he had also been admitted to the lunatic asylum at Devizes on three separate occasions, although he was not known to be violent.

Unable to consider Turner's mental state, the inquest jury returned a verdict of wilful murder against him and he was committed for trial at the Assizes. He didn't have long to wait since the next Wiltshire Assizes were in January 1897. By that time, he had been medically examined and found to be completely insane, and, judged unfit to plead, was ordered to be detained during Her Majesty's pleasure.

Bath

On 17 December 1925, five-year-old Dennis Evans of Bath, Somerset, was suffering from a very heavy cold and his mother decided to put him to bed early, leaving a gas fire burning in his room to keep him warm. Before long, she heard her son screaming and ran to see what the matter was.

Dennis had climbed out of bed and walked to the fireplace to peer up the chimney. His pyjamas came into contact with the lighted gas fire and burst into a ball of flames. 'I wanted to see Father Christmas,' he told his mother, shortly before dying from the effects of his burns.

Bristol

Priscilla Jenkins lived at Penn Street, St Paul's, as did William and Sarah Priddes and their family and Mrs Murphy. On 23 December 1883, Priscilla heard a commotion outside their house and, looking out of her window, saw Mrs Murphy, an epileptic, lying in the street in the throes of a fit. She was being supported by William Priddes and Priscilla rushed to help him.

With the assistance of another neighbour, Priscilla and William carried Mrs Murphy upstairs to her room. Later that day, Sarah Priddes noticed her husband rubbing his arm and asked him if he had hurt it. William dismissed her concerns, saying that he had just scratched himself, but, on Christmas Day, he asked his wife for some hot water to bathe his arm.

Sarah bathed it for him and, noticing that it looked slightly swollen, put a poultice on it. During that night, William himself suffered a fit but, although Sarah begged him to go to the Infirmary, he refused. On Boxing Day, his arm was so badly swollen and inflamed that she took matters into her own hands and procured a cab to take him there in spite of his protests.

Forty-seven-year-old William died at half-past eight that evening and house surgeon Mr Penny found that he had blood poisoning, arising from a human bite on his upper arm.

Bristol Royal Infirmary, 1910. (Author's collection)

Coroner Mr H.S. Wasbrough held an inquest at the Bristol General Hospital, at which Priscilla Jenkins recalled seeing William start as he was carrying Mrs Murphy upstairs, as if she had bitten or scratched him. The jury returned a verdict that '... death was due to blood poisoning resulting from an accidental bite inflicted by a woman whilst in a fit.'

Radstock

On Christmas Day 1876, Mr Coombs tried to shoot a blackbird in his garden. The gun failed to fire and Coombs took it back into his house at Radstock, Somerset, telling his wife that it was loaded but that he was unable to fire it. The gun normally hung on the wall, out of reach of the children, but now Mrs Coombs was afraid to touch it and simply stood it in a corner.

A little later, Mr and Mrs Coombs went out to see relatives, leaving their ten-year-old twin sons alone at home. A favourite pastime for the boys was detonating the heads of Lucifer matches in their toy pistol and, spotting their father's gun standing in the kitchen, they tried to do the same with a real gun. John tried first but failed. He went to wash his hands and his brother, Francis, picked up the gun and managed to fire it. Sadly, he shot his brother through the left loin and John died from his injuries three hours later.

At the subsequent inquest on John's death, deputy coroner Mr R. Biggs told the jury that blaming his twin brother was pointless. Although the jury fell short of recommending any legal action for negligence against John's parents, in returning a verdict of 'accidental death' they asked the coroner to strongly reprimand them for leaving the children alone in the house with a loaded gun.

Gloucester

Frederick Harris of Morpeth Street, Gloucester, was seriously ill and, on 22 December 1929, he was admitted to hospital. He was not expected to return home.

On Christmas Eve, a relative called at Harris's home, but, although Mrs Harris and her son and daughter should have been in, there was no response to the man's knocks. Eventually he broke into the house and found three bodies in an upstairs bedroom.

Mary Emma Harris, aged forty-three, her daughter Dora, aged twenty-two and her eighteen-year-old son George lay on a bed. The room had been carefully sealed with felt and sticky tape and a stove, ring and gas jet were all turned on but unlit, discharging deadly gas into the room. Downstairs was an empty bottle of wine containing a little powdery sediment and one of three empty glasses in the bedroom also contained traces of powder. The family doctor would later tell an inquest that he had given Mrs Harris four tablets of morphia for her husband and that he had also prescribed sleeping powders for her after she had a nervous breakdown.

Mrs Harris left two letters, one of which was addressed to her mother-in-law. It read: 'We must be there to meet dear Fred. We loved each other so. I am sure dear Dora and George would never get over the loss of us both. I am so sorry. God bless us all. No one will ever know what it has cost me to write this.' Relatives of the family stated that the family were exceptionally close and loving and that Mrs Harris often said that she didn't know if she could live without her husband.

The cause of all three deaths was gas poisoning and no tests were performed to establish whether or not any of the deceased was drugged. Hearing that, following her breakdown, any strain might have unhinged Mary Harris's reason, the inquest jury concluded that she committed suicide whilst of unsound mind and that her son and daughter died from gas poisoning, there being no evidence to show how it was administered.

Fifty-three-year-old Frederick Harris is believed to have died early in 1930.

Batheaston

Eighteen-year-old Mary Holloway, who was a servant at Old House Farm, Batheaston in Somerset, died on Christmas Day 1892 from serious burns received two days earlier. Farmer Charles Milsom Smith told an inquest that he and his wife heard a crash coming from the farm kitchen and when Smith went to investigate, he found Mary Holloway enveloped in flames.

Smith rushed Mary outside and rolled her on a bed of turnip greens until the fire was fully extinguished. However, by then

Mary had received such terrible burns to the lower half of her body that she died in hospital on Christmas morning. It was thought that the paraffin in a lamp in the kitchen had become heated due to the wick being turned up too high, causing the lamp to explode.

The inquest jury returned a verdict of accidental death.

Devonport

Mrs Parnell of Devonport, Plymouth, gave birth to a baby shortly before Christmas 1875 and, after the birth, her mother offered to help her around the house. On 23 December, the elderly lady made a batch of nourishing broth, which was given to Mrs Parnell and the nurse who was attending her confinement, along with the charwoman and Mrs Parnell's three-year-old daughter, Susanna Ellen Parnell.

Mrs Parnell and the nurse found the broth too bitter and each ate only a few mouthfuls. Even so, both were violently sick afterwards, while Mrs Parnell's mother, daughter and the charwoman, who ate much more of the soup, became terribly ill with violent stomach cramps and vomiting. While the two women ultimately recovered, Susanna died on Christmas Eve and doctors determined that her death resulted from eating deadly poisonous monkshood, which the child's grandmother accidentally mistook for parsley and added to the broth.

Long Ashton

On Christmas Eve 1885, ten-year-old Edward Light was found at Long Ashton, Somerset, having been missing from home for six days. Edward told his rescuers, Mr Bryant and Mr Cook, that he had run away from home because he had spent his school money. Some boys had pushed him into a pool and he had taken his wet boots off, but it was so cold that his feet had swollen and he was unable to get them back on. Chilled to the bone, he clambered inside a hollow tree on the Ashton Court estate to try and get warm but got stuck.

Although he could lie down inside the tree, he was unable to extricate himself. All he could do was put one hand through a hole in the trunk and wave it in the hope of attracting attention. On the first day, he had eaten some orange peel from his pocket but, since then, had eaten or drunk nothing.

Every time a cart had passed on the nearby lane, he had shouted for help but nobody answered his desperate cries until 24 December, when some children playing on the lane finally heard his shouts.

Light, who was said to be 'reduced almost to a skeleton', was rushed to the hospital at the Bedminster Union Workhouse. He was first given liquid food and then gradually weaned onto a light diet and, by the end of the first week in January 1887, was said to be well on the way to recovery. His legs were still swollen and his feet affected by frostbite, and doctors thought that it would be some time before he could walk again.

Sydling St Nicholas

As carter George King passed the cottage in Sydling St Nicholas, Dorset, occupied by Herbert and Emily Croad on Boxing Day 1892, he heard groans coming from an upstairs room. Unable to get into the house, King called for assistance and several men from the village tried without success to break in.

Eventually, Emily Croad's brother was called and, having forced open the back door with a crowbar, he went upstairs. There he found his sister lying on the bed covered in blood, her neck, face and hands slashed. Herbert lay on the bedroom floor, his throat cut and a bloody razor clutched in his hand. Both Herbert and Emily were still alive but very seriously injured.

The Croads were known to have been suffering from depression in recent months. Emily was particularly badly affected, so much so that Herbert had been advised to put her into the asylum. Herbert, who was devoted to his wife, was most unwilling, telling people that he had saved a little money and wanted to enjoy it with Emily first.

Herbert Croad died within a couple of hours but Emily lingered on, although little hope was held out for her recovery. At the inquest on Herbert's death held in the village by coroner Mr A.G. Symonds, the jury recorded a verdict of 'suicide while temporarily insane.' Emily survived the incident – as she was known to have been suicidal, it was widely believed that she had somehow persuaded her devoted husband that they should die together.

Bristol

Without the knowledge of his parents, fourteen-year-old George Parsons Pritchard bought a revolver from a shop and, on Christmas Eve 1888, he and a friend locked themselves in the loft of a brewery, with the intention of firing a few practice shots.

The boys fixed up a cigarette box for a target and were about to start shooting when George's companion heard noises in the street outside and suggested that they waited until the coast was clear. As George held the revolver and amused himself by looking into one of the chambers, it suddenly went off, shooting George through one eye and killing him instantly.

Bristol coroner Mr Wasbrough opened an inquest immediately after Christmas and the jury returned a verdict of 'accidental death', adding a rider condemning the shopkeeper who had sold the gun to Pritchard. Wasbrough agreed, saying that it seemed very reprehensible that a schoolboy should be able to go into a shop and purchase a deadly weapon without any questions being asked.

Trowbridge

Commercial traveller Edward Charles Ingram Richards met his colleague Samuel Gay (or Gray) on the evening of 23 December 1925. The men were representatives for Usher's Brewery and after calling on hotels in the Bath area, collecting orders and payments, they had supper before heading home to Trowbridge in Wiltshire. The weather had deteriorated and it was snowing heavily, thus Richards didn't arrive home until the early hours of Christmas Eve.

Richards shared his house in Victoria Road with Walter Stourton and his wife, who were sleeping soundly when they heard him shouting from the garden. Thinking that he had lost his key, Walter called that the back door was open but Richards wanted Walter to come downstairs.

Walter found Richards lying on his back in the garden with a head wound, clutching a recently fired revolver and claiming to have been shot. 'It was two men,' he told Walter, clutching his stomach and writhing in agony. He died within minutes of reaching hospital and a post-mortem examination revealed three wounds on the left-hand side of his head, along with a single bullet wound, which had perforated a lung and his heart.

The police started their investigations at the barracks of the Royal Horse Artillery, where they found that two bombardiers had been unaccountably absent at the time of the shooting. When the police discovered that one of them knew Richards and his normal routine, they were taken in for further questioning and, when a spot of fresh blood was found on a raincoat belonging to one of them, twenty-year-old Ian Ronald Maxwell Stewart and twenty-three-year-old Ignatius Emmanuel Napthall Trebitsch Lincoln (aka John Lincoln) were charged with wilful murder.

At their trial at the Wiltshire Assizes in January 1926, there was insufficient evidence to convict Stewart, who was discharged and immediately charged with robbery with violence. Knowing that Richards would be unable to pay the cash he received from his customers into his office because of the Christmas holidays, the two men broke into his house, lying in wait with the intention of robbing him. They shared half a bottle of brandy and had just started to make inroads on a crate of beer when the back door opened and a man's voice said, 'The game's up!'

A shot was fired and Lincoln ran through the house to the front door. Unable to unlock it, he went to the back door and poked his gun round the edge of it, firing three times in rapid succession. Although he hadn't aimed the gun and couldn't see where he was firing, Lincoln said that he 'accidentally' shot Richards as he fled through the garden trying to make his escape.

Lincoln's defence counsel insisted that his client was guilty of manslaughter rather than murder, since he was befuddled by alcohol and in fear for his life at the time of the shooting and hadn't aimed at Richards, so couldn't have intended to kill him. However, the jury disagreed and found Lincoln guilty of wilful murder.

Stewart's charge was again dismissed and he was then charged with burglary and eventually sentenced to fourteen years' penal servitude. Lincoln's death sentence was appealed but he was executed by Thomas Pierrepoint at Shepton Mallet Prison on 2 March 1926.

Bristol

Although the theatre doors didn't open until seven o'clock in the evening, on 27 December 1869 people formed long queues outside the New Theatre Royal at Bristol to see the Christmas pantomime, *Robinson Crusoe*. Some arrived as early as four o'clock in the afternoon and by six o'clock, the steep narrow gangway leading to the pit and gallery was crammed with hundreds of people.

As the doors opened and the crowd stampeded into the theatre, a woman was seen to trip and fall in the doorway. Several people tripped over her, while those behind continued to push for entrance, unaware that there was an obstruction ahead, scrambling over the fallen in their desperation to secure seats for the performance. Eventually, the police resorted to shouting 'Fire!' to try and clear the crowds.

By the time anyone could get to help them, twenty-three the atregoers were unconscious and fourteen at the very bottom of the pile were dead. Fearful of the consequences of cancelling the performance, the theatre manager had the six women, four men and four children carried to the refreshment room, while the injured were rushed to The Bristol Royal Infirmary, where a further four people died.

At an inquest held by coroner Mr H.S. Wasbrough, the jury recorded verdicts of accidental death on Mary Helen Sherwood (16), Thomas Marchant (19), Eliza Lucas (18), Patrick Donovan (15), Alfred Kew (18), Thomas Pearson (21), Samuel Hill (12), John Davis (14), Henry Charles Vining, George Potter (11), Ellen Jones (15), Sarah Ann Bilby (18), Elizabeth Hall (52), Catherine Brewer (16), Joseph Smith (15) , Charles Pring (18), William Samuel Alden (21) and Charles Talbot. All eighteen victims were either crushed or suffocated.

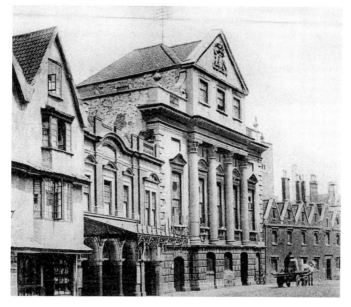

Theatre Royal, Bristol, 1905. (Author's collection)

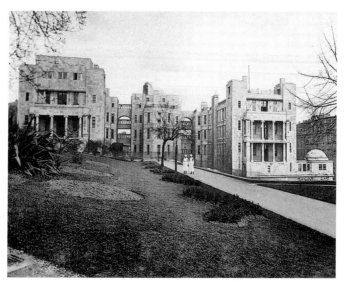

Bristol Royal Infirmary. (Author's collection)

Falmouth

When Albert Bateman didn't return home on Christmas Eve 1942, his wife went to look for him, finding his tobacconists shop in Falmouth, Cornwall, locked up. Concerned, Mrs Bateman contacted the police, who forced the shop door and found sixty-one-year-old Albert lying dead behind the counter. Although he had been battered to death rather than shot, a Webley revolver lay on the counter, which Mrs Bateman confirmed did not belong to her husband.

The police traced the ownership of the gun to Falmouth Docks, where they were told that a man named Gordon Horace Trenoweth had ready access to it. Trenoweth was a married man with five children, who was known to the police for refusing to support his wife. Mrs Trenoweth had lived in a mental institution since 1941 and her husband had recently served a prison sentence for defaulting on his payments for her maintenance.

Trenoweth was arrested at his parents' house in the early hours of Christmas Day, when he was found to have two packs of cigarettes in his possession, along with a torn banknote that had been repaired with a piece of paper bearing Bateman's shop letterhead. Later tests showed fibres from his jacket on the revolver and traces of gun oil in his pocket, as well as bloodstains of the same blood group as Bateman.

Although Trenoweth's father, sister and a man he approached looking for a job all gave him an alibi for the time of the murder, when Trenoweth was tried at the Exeter Assizes, the jury chose to believe the forensic evidence and the testimony from two witnesses, who stated that he had been spending money freely on the night of the murder. They found Trenoweth guilty, although they recommended mercy. The recommendation was not heeded, since Gordon Trenoweth became the last person ever to be hanged at Exeter Prison, keeping his appointment with executioner Thomas Pierrepoint on 6 April 1943.

TWO

SOUTH EAST

Polegate, near Eastbourne

By Christmas 1889, forty-four-year-old Mary Ann Taylor had been a widow for three years and had turned to alcohol to help her to cope. She and her late husband had produced ten children between them, most of whom were still dependent on their mother for support. Hence Mary Ann ran a small general provisions shop at Polegate, East Sussex, living over the premises.

On the night of Boxing Day 1889, Samuel 'Bertie' Taylor came home and found his mother lying on the sofa rather tipsy. He kissed her goodnight and went to bed but just thirty minutes later he heard one of his sisters shout, 'Oh, mother, you are hurting me.' Samuel went to see what was happening and as he walked downstairs he met his sister Kate. Her throat was gushing blood and, unable to speak, she pointed upstairs.

When Bertie reached the bedrooms, he found his mother with an open razor in her hands. He took it from her and in distress she begged him, 'Bertie, kill me.' Bertie could see his sisters, twelve-year-old Eleanor Ethel and fourteen-year-old Caroline Harriet lying dead on their beds, their throats cut.

'Have you done the others?' he asked his mother.

'No, but I was just going to,' she replied.

Bertie fetched a neighbour, who bandaged Kate's throat to staunch the bleeding. She was taken to the Princess Alice Hospital in Eastbourne, where she eventually recovered. Meanwhile, her mother was arrested and taken to the police cells at Hailsham.

Broadmoor Criminal Lunatic Asylum, 1906. (Author's collection)

Mary Ann Taylor was tried for the wilful murder of her two daughters at Lewes Assizes in March 1890. Although Bertie insisted that he smelled alcohol on his mother's breath when he kissed her goodnight, a doctor who examined her at the police station said that, although she smelled of beer, she was not drunk when she murdered her daughters. The jury found her guilty but insane and she was ordered to be detained during Her Majesty's pleasure and sent to Broadmoor Criminal Lunatic Asylum.

Bagshot

When sixteen-year-old Emily Jane 'Janey' Popejoy began working as a maid for Mrs Camilla Nicholls at Kensington in October 1896, she was a fine, strapping girl who had only suffered two days' illness in her life. When Janey was sent home to her mother at Bagshot, Surrey, on Christmas Eve 1897, she weighed just four and a half stones, had a broken nose and a broken finger and was bruised black and blue from head to toe.

So serious was Janey's condition that a magistrate was summoned on Boxing Day to take her deposition. However, Janey died just as he arrived, leaving only her statement to PC Nunn that her mistress was responsible for her condition.

West Surrey coroner Mr G.F. Roumieu conducted an inquest, at which numerous witnesses testified to seeing Janey beaten with a brush, hammer, stick or umbrella or being kicked by Mrs Nicholls. According to witnesses, Janey was always so hungry that she would pick up discarded food from the street and eat it.

More than one witness told the inquest that they had offered to 'have it out' with Mrs Nicholls but said that Janey pleaded with them not to, saying that it would make her situation worse. Janey was unable to leave her employment because she had no money to escape.

The inquest returned a verdict of manslaughter against Camilla Nicholls, who was tried by Mr Justice Phillimore at the Central Criminal Court in May 1898. The defence insisted that Janey was unclean, with dirty habits, as well as being immoral and lacking in intelligence. If this was the case then why did Mrs Nicholls continue employing her, asked the counsel for the prosecution?

It took the jury only minutes to find Camilla Nicholls guilty of manslaughter and Phillimore sentenced her to seven years' imprisonment. She fainted on hearing her fate and was taken from court by hansom cab to Wormwood Scrubs Prison and later transferred to Aylesbury, where she served her sentence.

Wavendon, near Newport Pagnell

The Wavendon House estate near Newport Pagnell, Buckinghamshire, had recently experienced significant losses at the hands of poachers. Hence, on Christmas Eve 1867, gamekeepers John White and Mr Farr were patrolling Wavendon Wood, looking for any signs of suspicious activity.

At about six o'clock in the evening, they came across James Inwood and William Emmerton out poaching. As soon as he realised they had been spotted, Inwood told Emmerton, 'Shoot 'em'. Emmerton replied that he would not and took to his heels, with Farr in pursuit. They had gone only 50 yards when a gunshot rang out and, turning, they saw White crumpling to the ground.

Farr and Emmerton ran back to help him, while Inwood ran off. 'Farr, I am a dead man and it's James Inwood that has shot me,' White gasped before dying.

An inquest on his death returned a verdict of wilful murder against Inwood, who was committed for trial at the next Buckinghamshire Assizes, where he appeared in March 1868. In spite of Inwood's insistence that his gun went off accidentally, Emmerton was the chief prosecution witness against him and the jury found him guilty of manslaughter. He was sentenced to twenty years' imprisonment.

Portsea

In the days before Christmas 1918, Mrs Smith was so worried about her son-in-law's strange behaviour that she tried to get him 'put away'. Twenty-eight-year-old Charles William Rose was unable to afford a home of his own, so he and his wife and two sons lived with Mrs Smith in Portsea, Hampshire. Mother and son-in-law didn't get on too well since Mrs Smith persisted in interfering and the tension between them was exacerbated by the fact that Rose had a terrible ear infection, which was dripping pus and causing him intolerable pain.

On Boxing Day, Rose was playing with his sons in the living room while his wife and her mother were busy in the kitchen. At about four o'clock in the afternoon, Rose joined them there and, taking his wife's hand, told her, 'I am going away. Your babies won't worry you anymore. You are a free woman.' Alarmed, Mrs Rose went to check on her children, finding Alfred Frederick, aged two, and his infant brother William James lying dead in bed in an upstairs room, their throats cut.

Rose was eventually found a couple of days later, sitting woefully on a park bench in Portsmouth. Although he initially gave the police a false name, he was soon identified and charged with two counts of wilful murder.

Tried at the Winchester Assizes, the main question for the jury was not whether Rose murdered his sons but his mental state at the time of the killings. Medical experts disagreed, some saying that they believed that Rose was sane, others suggesting that the painful ear infection, coupled with lack of sleep, had tipped Rose over the edge into insanity.

The jury were later to say that they couldn't comprehend that anyone in his right mind could commit so heinous and brutal a

The judge and escort outside Winchester Assizes, 1909. (Author's collection)

crime on two innocent young children. Hence they found Rose guilty but insane and he was ordered to be detained as a criminal lunatic until His Majesty's pleasure be known.

Newport, Isle of Wight

Convict Thomas Gilbert was serving a seven-year sentence in Parkhurst Prison, Newport. Classed as a lunatic, he was confined to a padded cell, which he decided to leave via a chimney flue on Christmas Day 1896.

Gilbert, who was thirty years old, was an ex-dragoon and was described in the contemporary newspapers as 'powerfully built' and 'a man of fine physique'. Dressed in his convict's uniform, he marched up to the guardhouse at the military barracks adjoining the prison. The guard challenged him, 'Friend or foe?' and, when Gilbert replied 'Friend' the guard assumed that he was one of the soldiers having a joke and let him pass into the barracks.

Gilbert stole a uniform and marched out again, much to the consternation of the people living near the prison, who were most unhappy to find that a dangerous madman was at large amongst them.

Fortunately, Gilbert was recaptured in Ryde on 26 December.

Parkhurst Prison, Isle of Wight. (Author's collection)

Greenhithe

Having been widowed in 1866, Elizabeth Henry supported herself and her children by keeping a grocer's shop in Greenhithe, Kent. The Henrys lived over the shop, as did Elizabeth's widowed sister, Frances Kempton, and a fifteen-year-old servant, Mary Poole, who was the daughter of the Henrys' next-door neighbours

On Christmas Day 1866, Elizabeth's parents spent the day with the family, leaving for London at half-past seven in the evening and taking their oldest granddaughter to stay with them for a few days. Soon afterwards, the Henry family retired to bed, where they slept soundly until the early hours of the next morning, when Frances Kempton woke to the smell of burning. She shouted up to her sister, who began waking the children, but they were so terrified that they ran away from her.

Frances was badly burned and, unable to escape the flames any other way, eventually jumped out of a window onto the roof of an outhouse 20 feet below. Although she was injured, she managed to alert neighbour Mr Poole, who got his wife and eight children out of his house and led them to safety.

A man on a pony volunteered to fetch the fire brigade but the animal refused to pass the fire, which caused a considerable delay.

Mrs Henry was heard shouting, 'For God's sake, save the children,' but there was no portable fire escape located anywhere near the area and Elizabeth, Mary Poole, four-year-old Bertie Henry and his six-month-old brother, Walter, perished in the blaze.

An inquest was opened and adjourned in the hope that Frances would be well enough to attend. The proceedings resumed when she was discharged from hospital, concluding on 10 January 1867 with verdicts that the deceased died in the fire but there was no evidence to suggest how the fire originated.

Purley

On Christmas Eve 1924, an Imperial Airways Ltd aeroplane bound for Paris crashed at Purley, Surrey, about a mile and a half from Croydon Aerodrome, from where it had taken off. The plane flew low over Purley before nose-diving towards the ground, crashing and bursting into flames.

Although rescue workers were quickly on the scene, the blaze was too intense and the pilot and seven passengers perished.

An inquest and a government inquiry were held into the accident. It was suggested by eyewitnesses that the pilot was attempting either to return to Croydon or to perform an emergency landing when the plane stalled. There were questions about a blocked petrol supply pipe but it was concluded that the fire-fighting efforts caused the blockage rather than the blockage causing the crash. The inquest jury returned verdicts of 'death by misadventure' and the inquiry cleared the pilot of blame for the accident, finding that the aircraft crashed due to an unknown mechanical defect and subsequent stall while an emergency landing was being attempted.

Redhill

William Arthur Hawley entered the 'Earlswood Asylum for Idiots' in Redhill, Surrey in May 1880, where he was said to have a voracious appetite and to be incapable of speaking or dressing himself. Nevertheless, he was put to work in the coconut mat-making shop, where he stayed for almost a year until his deteriorating physical health prevented him from working.

Earlswood Asylum. (Author's collection)

On Christmas Eve 1885, Hawley died, aged twenty, after a bout of vomiting. A post-mortem examination showed that he had a blockage in his intestines, consisting of human hair, horse hair, coconut fibre and dead leaves. The mass weighed in excess of 2¼lb and completely obstructed Hawley's stomach.

He was known to pull out his own hair and died almost completely bald. Doctors surmised that he must have been swallowing hair and other things for many years and determined that his death resulted from exhaustion, caused by constant indigestion.

Rainham

On Christmas Eve 1889, forty-two-year-old James Blowfield and his thirteen-year-old son Albert went to Stranger's Creek, near the mouth of the Medway in Kent, to get some oysters for Christmas fare. While they were busy at the oyster beds, they failed to notice the rising tide and were soon cut off from the mainland.

When he realised their predicament, Blowfield attempted to drive his horse and cart back through the deep water. Sadly, the cart overturned and both he and his son were drowned, as was the horse. A man who accompanied them on the trip managed to swim ashore.

Aldershot

In Aldershot, the boys in the Royal Artillery Mounted Band were eagerly anticipating a furlough for Christmas 1904. They were singing and shouting with excitement when their rowdy behaviour disturbed Bandsman Frederick Turner, whose sleeping quarters were just above the barrack room.

In a blind fury, Turner stormed downstairs and, seizing the first boy he could lay his hands on, proceeded to give him a thrashing which left him unconscious. When Turner attacked him, Hemming was holding a riding boot with a spur in his hand and he tried to defend himself with it. Turner was hit in the side and, when he later complained of pain, was taken to hospital where he was found to be suffering from an internal rupture. He died on Boxing Day.

An inquest later returned a verdict of 'death from misadventure', the jury exonerating Hemming from blame as they considered that he struck Turner only after extreme provocation.

Shipton-on-Cherwell

The train travelling from London to Oxford, Birmingham and the North on Christmas Eve 1874 was packed with people going to spend the festive season with their families.

As the train neared Shipton-on-Cherwell, Oxfordshire, a metal tire on a third-class carriage broke, causing it to leave the rails. It skidded along for some 300 yards before swerving left down a 20-foot embankment.

The carriage was 'smashed to atoms' and the following carriages plunged after it. 'The crimsoned snow on the brink of the embankment told terribly what was to be expected of an inspection of the carriage . . . blood and brains were bespattered all over the interior, interspersed with portions of human hair and on the floor, amid the wreck of wood and torn cushions, the broken glass lay stiffly frozen in blood,' reported a contemporary newspaper.

Local people pitched in to help the wounded and the dead were taken to nearby Hampton Gay Paper Mill to await identification. When the rescue operation was complete, there were thirty-four fatalities, with a further sixty-nine people injured.

The terrible railway accident at Shipton-on-Cherwell: identifying the dead at Hampton Gay Paper Mill. (Author's collection)

An inquiry into the accident discovered that, once the driver was alerted to the presence of the broken tire by a passenger, he applied the brakes and reversed the engine. Unfortunately, the carriages did not slow down and the third-class carriage was crushed by the weight of those behind, which then jumped off the rails in consequence. Had the driver shut off the steam and applied the brakes gradually, it was believed that the accident could have been avoided.

High Wycombe

Inmates of the Wycombe Union Workhouse in Buckinghamshire were given a special dinner on Christmas Day 1876. Eighty-year-old pauper Thomas Vyse was known to eat very quickly and his throat muscles were constricted by disease. Hence his roast beef, roast pork and vegetables were cut up into very small pieces before he was given his plate of food. Even so, Vyse choked and the wards attendants were unable to clear whatever was blocking his throat.

A post-mortem examination later revealed that, rather than chewing his food, he had simply swallowed it and his throat was completely stopped with solid pieces of meat.

Portsmouth

On Christmas Eve 1836, widow Ellen Oldson was given an early gift of a bottle of rum. She returned home from her job selling poultry in Portsea and Portsmouth, Hampshire, and made a point of asking her neighbour to call her early on Christmas morning as she wanted to go to Mass.

The neighbour heard Ellen chopping sticks at ten o'clock in the evening but when he knocked on her door at just after seven o'clock on Christmas morning, there was no reply. Thinking that she had already gone to Mass, he left, but by eleven o'clock, when he had neither seen nor heard anyone stirring next door and his knocks drew no response, he fetched a ladder and put it up to the bedroom window.

Ellen Oldson was lying on the floor, completely incinerated. Her five-year-old son, William, was bent over his mother, apparently trying to rouse her and almost suffocated by smoke. A doctor was called immediately but William lived only a few hours.

An inquest found that Ellen had burned to death, the jury presuming that she had accidentally set herself on fire while drunk. William died from suffocation, arising from the burning of his mother's body and clothes.

Greenhithe

On Boxing Day 1827, *Vigilant* of Greenwich was sailing from Gravesend when she capsized off Greenhithe, Kent. Witnesses stated that the boat was under sail at the time and seemed top heavy, falling victim to a sudden squall.

Three men clung to the bottom of the overturned boat and the crew from a nearby brig went to rescue them. As they neared, one of the survivors slipped off the boat and drifted away.

The two men clinging to the boat were saved and the third man was found floating some distance away. He was barely alive and although surgeon Mr Tomlin laboured for more than two hours to try and revive him, he had sustained a ruptured trachea, which proved fatal.

The dead man was identified as Mr Martin from Deptford, who was travelling with his wife, two daughters and an uncle, and there were three other passengers on board *Vigilant*, along with the ship's crew. At the time of the inquest on Mr Martin's death, at which the jury returned a verdict of 'accidental death by drowning', no other bodies had been recovered. The ship had sunk in about eight fathoms of water and it was thought that the remaining passengers and crew were still trapped in the hold.

Hove

On Christmas Eve 1864, John Cooms was entertaining a few neighbours at his home at Hove, East Sussex. As a child, Cooms accidentally drank a quantity of turpentine, which caused his feet to wither and die, hence he was known as 'No Legs'.

The beer and spirits flowed, followed by hot elderberry wine and at one point Joseph Sharp went outside and howled like a wolf. Cooms told him to be quiet, a suggestion which Sharp did

Church Road, Hove. (Author's collection)

not take too kindly. He and Cooms argued and, when Cooms slapped Sharp's face, Sharp pushed him off his chair onto the floor.

Some people objected to Sharp hitting a disabled man but he took no notice of their protests until eventually John Bishop and John Dyke forcibly pinned him against a wall and tried to persuade him to go home.

It was only then that Bishop noticed that Cooms had armed himself with a gun. He asked Cooms to surrender his weapon but Cooms told him, 'If you don't get out of the way, I will shoot you!' Bishop didn't need warning twice and, just as he was leaving the room, he heard Cooms say, 'Now Mr ★★★★★★★ Joe, I'm ready for you.'

There was a loud bang followed by a thud, as if a man had fallen onto the floor. PC Bristowe was patrolling his beat only yards away and bravely raced into the house, disarming Cooms, who was still holding the gun. When Bishop got back inside, Bristowe was holding Cooms by the hands, while Sharp lay in a spreading pool of blood, a bullet wound just above his left eye.

Cooms was charged with wilful murder, appearing at the Lewes Assizes in March 1865. Both Dyke and Bishop testified that Sharp was very drunk and notoriously short-tempered and that he was 'using Cooms very cruelly'. He pushed him off the bed, punched him, jumped on his chest two or three times and made use of the most profane language. Bishop recalled pulling Sharp away from Cooms, adding that he and Dyke were hit two or three times by Sharp. Even as they pinned him to the wall, Sharp struggled furiously and Bishop was sure that if he could have got to Cooms, he would have done him a serious injury.

Part of the way through the trial, the presiding judge interrupted, asking the prosecution if they truly believed that they could prove murder and the prosecution conceded that perhaps they couldn't.

It was suggested that Cooms should plead guilty to manslaughter, which he did. In considering his sentence, the judge took into account Cooms's brutal treatment by the victim, which constituted extreme provocation. Nevertheless, it was impossible to disregard the fact that it was unacceptable to go around shooting anyone who upset you and Cooms was sentenced to twelve months' imprisonment with hard labour.

Maidstone

On the afternoon of Christmas Day 1879, a party of young people from Thurnham went to skate on the lake at the Old Mill at Leeds, Kent. After a pleasant afternoon, George Barney ventured towards the end of the pond at which the stream entered, where the water was barely frozen.

When he fell into the pool, another skater, George Cheeseman, immediately went to his aid but he too fell into the icy water, as did Ellen Cheeseman, her younger brother and two more of the party. Their desperate screams brought people rushing to the scene and a man named Thomas Hughes held out a hop pole from the water's edge and succeeded in rescuing four of the skaters, but sixteen-year-old George and his fourteen-year-old sister, Ellen, were carried under the ice by the stream's current and it was almost two hours before their bodies could be recovered.

Bexley

On Christmas morning 1807 eighteen-year-old maid Edith Agnes Wood was left in the house at Bexley, Kent, while the family she worked for went to church. She was playing with the dog in front of the fire when her long skirts suddenly caught alight.

Edith screamed frantically and her desperate cries so frightened her sister, who was with her, that instead of trying to put out the flames, the girl ran to her bedroom, locked the door and hid under the bed. Meanwhile, in a state of terror and sheer panic, Edith ran round like a mad woman, setting fire to carpets, curtains and furniture as she did.

Eventually, neighbours heard the commotion and managed to break into the house and extinguish the flames. Their intervention came too late for Edith, who died later that day.

Oxford

Sixty-four-year-old Martha Harris was the widow of a railway contractor but, after her husband's death, she was left penniless.

She was persuaded to enter the Workhouse but hated it so much that she left to take her chances in the outside world, renting a small room near Oxford county gaol.

She seemed entirely dependent on what food she could pick up from the streets and, on Christmas Day 1867, was so hungry that she sold her petticoats for a penny, with which she purchased a piece of bread.

A couple of days later, a neighbour found Martha dead on the floor, almost completely naked. She wore just a single stocking and a dirty rag tied around her neck and clung to a rickety old chair that was the only furniture in the room. There was no fire in the grate and Martha was freezing and so hungry that she had gnawed her own arm.

Lewes

On Christmas Eve 1836 it began to snow very heavily in the South East and the blizzards continued throughout Christmas Day, when gale force winds created huge snowdrifts up to 50 feet high. At the top of Cliffe Hills in Lewes, the snow formed a massive overhanging shelf and, on 27 December, the shelf collapsed, the resulting avalanche completely crushing the seven cottages that lay beneath it.

'The mass appeared to strike the houses first at the base, heaving them upwards, and then breaking over them like a gigantic wave,' wrote the *Sussex Weekly Advertiser*, 'There was nothing but a mound of pure white.'

People immediately began to dig through the mountain of snow to try and get to those trapped beneath it, while lookouts were posted to warn them of any further falls and indeed, there was a second fall, which buried many of the rescue workers. Fortunately most escaped without injury.

William Geer (82), Joseph Wood (15), Mary Taylor (42), Phoebe Barnden (42), Maria Bridgman (28), Mary Bridgman (11), Jane Boaks (25) and Susan Hayward (34) perished in the avalanche and many more people were injured. The cottages were completely destroyed and The Snowdrop Inn was later built on the site.

Aylesbury

On 23 December 1904, the Great Central newspaper train was heading towards Manchester when it failed to slow down for a curve on the London side of Aylesbury Station in Buckinghamshire. It was derailed and, minutes later, a Great Central passenger train from Manchester – fortunately carrying no passengers – approached from the opposite direction and ploughed into the wreckage.

Driver Daniel Summers (36), firemen Joseph (or Josiah) Stanton (25) and George William Masters (29) died instantly, while driver Joseph Barnshaw (32) was trapped in the wreckage and suffered severe scalds from the steam. He died in hospital the following day.

The train from Marylebone was carrying meat, fish, fruit and Christmas parcels and hampers but its main cargo was newspapers. There was immense competition for circulation between the national newspapers, which led to the London-based newspapers trying to ensure that their publications reached the Manchester area as early as possible, to allow them to compete with the *Manchester Guardian*. Thus the driver, Barnshaw was under pressure to complete the journey as quickly as possible and a later inquiry suggested that he was unfamiliar with the route.

Aylesbury railway disaster, 23 December 1904. (Author's collection)

There was a mandatory speed limit of 15mph on the curve and it was estimated that Barnshaw was driving at around 50mph. However, it was extremely foggy at the time of the accident and an inquest concluded that the fog was so dense that he probably hadn't realised his exact position on the line and so could not be held culpably negligent. A verdict of accidental death was returned on all four victims.

Browndown

Royal Marines Henry Spurrier and James Whatmore were billeted together in barracks at Browndown, Hampshire. The two men were good friends, so much so that on Christmas Eve 1898, Spurrier took Whatmore's stint of guard duty for him.

By midnight, everyone in the sleeping quarters was in bed but at a quarter to three on Christmas morning, Private Wright, was awakened by voices and saw Spurrier and Whatmore sitting comfortably in armchairs on either side of the fire. They were apparently conversing amicably until Whatmore said, 'You have done it now,' and suddenly slumped forwards in his chair. Wright could see that Whatmore's back was bleeding and raised the alarm but Whatmore died almost instantly from a single stab wound that pierced his heart.

Spurrier walked calmly and quietly out into the barrack yard, where he was seen to throw a knife into the moat. Asked why he had stabbed his comrade, Spurrier seemed totally unconcerned, claiming that he did it to 'buck him up a bit'.

The civilian police were called and Spurrier was taken into custody. According to all who saw him, he seemed dazed and confused, described by Superintendent Hatt as 'totally lost.' An inquest was held into Whatmore's death but Spurrier suffered an epileptic fit at the start of the proceedings and so didn't hear the jury return a verdict of wilful murder against him.

He was tried at the Hampshire Assizes in February 1899. The court heard that Spurrier was a good, kind-hearted man and an excellent soldier, with five years' service in the regiment. However, for about six weeks prior to Whatmore's murder, Spurrier's behaviour had been decidedly strange and naval surgeon Mr P.V. Jackson thought it highly possible that he stabbed

Whatmore while having a fit, attributing his confusion afterwards to the aftermath of a seizure.

Spurrier's mother was called to talk about the extensive family history of epilepsy and insanity. Spurrier's father was an epileptic who died in a lunatic asylum in 1896, and he had two sisters, one of whom was confined in an asylum, described as 'hopelessly insane', the other having died in an asylum earlier that month while in the throes of an epileptic fit. Medical witnesses were agreed that Spurrier suffered from inherited insanity and epilepsy and he was found not guilty on the grounds of insanity and ordered to be detained during Her Majesty's pleasure.

New Brompton

On Christmas Eve 1881, Mrs Ratcliffe of New Brompton, Kent, popped out to do a little last-minute shopping. Since she wasn't expecting to be long, she left her three children at home.

She had not been gone long when neighbours noticed smoke coming from the house. Unable to get any response to their knocking on the door and shouting, they forced open the door, finding the house on fire.

Eighteen-month-old Alice was removed from one of the downstairs rooms but sadly she had burned to death. Upstairs, neighbours found six-year-old Francis and four-year-old Maude, both of whom were alive when carried from the building. Sadly, both died from the effects of smoke within a few minutes.

The fire was thought to have been started by a piece of lighted coal flying out of the grate, although the only open fire in the house was guarded.

Guildford

It was a Christmas tradition at the Royal Surrey County Hospital to have a game of snapdragon to amuse and entertain those patients forced to spend the festive season on the wards. The game involved taking a dish of raisins or similar fruits, which were placed in a shallow dish and covered with spirits. The alcohol was then lit, burning with a spectacular blue flame and the game was to snatch the fruits from the fire and eat them.

On Christmas night 1893, a group of carol singers toured the hospital. On the men's ward, the lights were lowered and house surgeon Charles Frier placed a dish of plums on a table, poured brandy over it and set it alight. It burned well for a while but then the flames began to dwindle. Mr Harrison, one of the carol singers, noticed Frier removing the cork from a bottle of methylated spirits and before Harrison could stop him, Frier poured the liquid over the still burning plums.

There was what Harrison described as a 'vaporous explosion'. Several children and members of staff were badly burned, including ten-year-old Archibald Lawrence Hooke, who later died from shock arising from his injuries. At the inquest on Hooke's death, Frier stated that he had organised the snapdragon the previous year and, having been shown what to do then, had done exactly the same this year. Methylated spirits was inflammable but not explosive, unless mixed with air, and he could only think that there must have been alcoholic vapour in the top of the bottle, which exploded when it came into contact with the naked flame.

The coroner remarked that snapdragon originated in pagan times and it should perhaps now be given up. The inquest jury concurred and, having condemned the hospital for allowing the game to take place on the ward, were rewarded with a promise from the chairman of the hospital that it would never do so again.

Grimsbury

In 1844, two young men walking along the banks of the River Cherwell in Oxfordshire on Christmas Day noticed a hole in the ice, with a boy's cap floating on the water. The men raised the alarm and before long the bodies of brothers Job and George Eaglestone, aged twelve and fourteen, were pulled from the water.

The two boys had been sent to deliver a gig to Banbury and were returning on foot. They were accompanied by seventeen-year-old John Green, who lived next door to their home in Wardington, and, since Green was missing, locals continued dragging the river until nightfall. Green's body was recovered when the dragging recommenced at first light on Boxing Day.

An inquest heard that the three boys had been seen sliding on the ice near Grimsbury Mill by a little boy, who tried to join them. However, one of the Eaglestone boys had shouted at him, calling him 'mutton head' and he had decided not to play after all. The inquest jury returned a verdict of 'accidentally drowned' on all three victims, the coroner remarking that it was extremely fortunate that there hadn't been a fourth.

Note: There are some discrepancies between various accounts of the tragedy in respect of the names of the Eaglestone brothers. They are referred to as Jacob, Job, Joshua, John and George but official records indicate that the correct names were Job and George.

Aldershot 🌿❄️🌿

In military establishments all over the country, discipline was always a little more liberal over Christmas and allowances were made for slight breaches of regulations. Such was the case at Aldershot in 1859, where the 2nd Battalion of the 24th Regiment and the Tower Hamlets Militia occupied the same permanent barracks. There was never any quarrel between the two units until Christmas Day, when a drunken squabble resulted in an all-out attack by the 2nd Battalion, who opened fire on the Tower Hamlets men killing one and seriously wounding three more.

It was customary for the officers to serve the men with Christmas dinner and there was plenty of alcohol to wash it down. By late afternoon, many of the men were intoxicated. Some of the Tower Hamlets men generously treated some of the 2nd Battalion to drinks but other members of the Battalion helped themselves uninvited to the drink bought by the Tower Hamlets men, who took exception.

A fight broke out and the Battalion men armed themselves with sticks, brooms, stones and even large lumps of coal. They outnumbered the Tower Hamlets men by almost six to one, and, as the Tower Hamlets men were getting soundly thrashed, many of them retreated to the safety of their rooms. A shout went up that they were fetching their rifles and, not to be outdone, the 2nd Battalion armed themselves and opened fire.

Private James King of the Militia was innocently warming himself by the fire when a pistol ball came through the door of his room and went straight through his abdomen. He died in agony a few hours later.

It was a wild and windy night and the officers were unaware of the fracas until the first shot was fired. They called in reinforcements and took all weapons and ammunition from both regiments, finding that no shots had been fired by the Tower Hamlets men. Around fifty of the 2nd Battalion were taken into custody but most were so drunk that they simply couldn't recall what had happened. There were so many witnesses to the shooting, each of whom had a completely different and often contradictory account of what he had seen.

An inquest on King's death was held at The Tilbury Hotel in Aldershot by coroner Samuel Chandler, at which the jury determined that the deceased was unlawfully killed by some person belonging to the 2nd Battalion but that there was insufficient evidence to determine who fired the fatal shot.

Littlemore

On Boxing Day 1890, seventy-five-year-old James Shouler died at Littlemore Asylum, Oxfordshire, where he was a patient.

On Christmas Day, he was dozing comfortably by the fire when he was called to the tea table. Shouler, who was a rather irritable man, rudely indicated with a profanity that he was quite happy where he was and had no intention of moving.

Attendant Frederick Bradbury went to 'persuade' Shouler to have his tea but Shouler picked up two large spoons and threw them at Bradbury. As he picked up a third, Bradbury tried to take it from him and the two men wrestled, falling onto the floor. Eventually, Shouler was physically carried to the table, where he ate his tea without further protest.

After Shouler's death, a post-mortem examination revealed that he had two dislocated ribs and an 'extraversion of blood' in his chest. However, the actual cause of his death was peritonitis, resulting from a very small hole in his intestines.

Coroner Mr Robinson held an inquest on Shouler's death, at which Bradbury downplayed the amount of physical force used in getting Shouler to the tea table. Inmate John Luckett, who assisted Bradbury to carry Shouler, stated that the warder knelt on Shouler and banged his head on the floor, prompting Shouler to protest, 'Why do you use an old fellow like me in this manner?' According to Luckett, Bradbury also boxed Shouler's ears.

The Asylum chaplain suggested that Luckett had been coached by another inmate and consequently his evidence was not reliable. The inquest jury returned an open verdict of 'death from peritonitis' and although they stopped short of blaming Bradbury, they recommended that he should be cautioned against using more force than necessary in dealing with his charges.

Teddington

As Mr and Mrs Reid of Teddington, Middlesex, finished wrapping the last of their presents on Christmas Eve 1929, they realised that an engine that they had purchased for one of their sons needed methylated spirits to run. Roderick Reid volunteered to go and buy some and, while he was out, his wife asked him to deliver some Christmas gifts.

When Mr Reid returned home at about eleven o'clock, the police and fire brigade were at his house and broke the tragic news that his wife was dead.

At an inquest held on 27 December, Reid explained to coroner Dr Crone that he hadn't yet told his two sons about their mother's fate. Ten-year-old John was called as a witness and questioned very carefully.

He told the inquest that he was in bed on Christmas Eve but was unable to sleep because he was waiting for Father Christmas to come. He smelled smoke and, when he got up to investigate, he saw it drifting down the hall and found his mother lying on

the bedroom floor, with some of her clothes on fire. John stated that the electric fire in his mother's room was broken, so he unplugged it. He then extinguished his mother's burning clothes, opened a window to clear the smoke, woke his brother and took him to a neighbour's house.

Thirty-nine-year-old Nora Reid had recently been suffering from bad bilious attacks and had complained of feeling faint at times. It was initially assumed that she had fainted and fallen onto the electric fire but a post-mortem examination revealed that she had severe heart disease and just happened to be near to the electric fire when she collapsed. The severe burns she incurred were incidental and the jury therefore returned a verdict of 'death from natural causes'.

Newington

Actress Catherine Ewins, who was more commonly known by her stage name Kittie Tyrrel, was appearing in a pantomime in Newington, Surrey. The cast had Christmas Day 1894 off, during which they indulged in the extra food and drink associated with the festive period.

On Boxing Day, Kittie played the part of a rat in 'Dick Whittington and his Cat'. One of her scenes called for her to sing and dance and, at the end, she moved into the wings and asked staff there to send for her husband Harry, who was working backstage. When Harry got to her, she seized his hand and pleaded, 'Harry, undo me, I'm dying.'

Harry immediately understood that his wife was complaining that her corsets were too tightly laced and set about rectifying the matter. However, his intervention came too late and Kittie died. A post-mortem examination showed that death was due to the effect of the tight lacing on the heart's action, which was recorded as 'death from syncope'.

THREE

LONDON

Lambeth

The afternoon performance of the Christmas pantomime on
Boxing Day 1858 was drawing to a close at the Victoria Theatre,
Lambeth and, by five o'clock, crowds of people were already
packing the stairs leading to the gallery, waiting to take their seats
for the evening show.

The contemporary newspapers stated that '. . . an unruly rabble
was packed nearly to suffocation on the stairs as far as the money-
taker's box, where a barrier impeded its further ascent and a
kindred rabble within the building was on the point of making its
exit into the open air.' In order to expedite the rapid movement
of crowds, the theatre management had arranged a different exit
route for the afternoon theatre-goers and had locked the doors to
the stairway.

At that point, someone noticed a strong smell of gas on the
staircase. Soon afterwards, there was a small explosion on the
second or third landing and people began shouting 'Fire!' Those at
the top of the stairs immediately began to try to move downwards,
while those at the very bottom of the staircase, who had no idea
that there was a problem, kept walking upstairs. People became
trapped between the two masses of people who were moving in
different directions. Some were trampled to the ground, some
crushed and others were unable to move in any direction and
were smothered. Some threw themselves over the balustrades
until gradually the people on the lower levels of the staircase real-

ised that there was a problem above. However, they themselves were unable to go backwards, due to the great number of people behind them who were still trying to get into the theatre.

When the crowds were finally dispersed and the police were able to get into the theatre, the grim task of dealing with the casualties began. At one stage, there were almost 100 seriously injured people but the final death toll was sixteen, all young men.

When it came to the inquests on the deceased, there seemed to be some confusion about what had prompted the shouts of 'Fire!' that acted as a catalyst to the tragedy. Some people believed that a person on the staircase had struck a match to light a cigar, which had caused a small explosion from the leaking gas. Others were of the opinion that somebody actually inside the theatre had struck a match and that, when the matchbox caught fire, it was thrown down and stamped out.

The coroner asked the jury if, in their opinion, anyone within the theatre had done anything deliberate to cause alarm, panic and eventual death, in which case they could be prosecuted for manslaughter supposing they could be traced. The jury determined that the deaths were accidental.

Croydon

On Boxing Day night 1896, Alfred Daws was having a party when his brother, George, suddenly burst into the house and excitedly announced that he had killed his wife. When his sister-in-law went to check his claim, she found Sarah Daws dead in her blood-drenched bed at her home in Oakwood Road, Croydon. She had been beaten about the head with a hammer and her throat had also been cut with a razor. Daws was arrested and charged with his wife's murder but seemed somewhat bewildered. He was normally a quiet, respectable man, who had a good relationship with his wife but who became violent under the influence of alcohol and, while drunk, had previously threatened to kill Sarah. Indeed, during June 1896, he was bound over by magistrates to keep the peace towards his wife for a period of

The Old Bailey (Central Criminal Court), London. (Author's collection)

six months, a sentence that only expired the previous week. The couple's neighbours were aware of no quarrel between them immediately before the murder but stated that Daws was drinking heavily that morning. When he was interviewed by the police, it was also obvious that he was delusional, believing that his wife was engaged in an intimate relationship with her stepson and also with the landlord of a local pub.

Tried for wilful murder at the Central Criminal Court in January 1897 and found guilty but insane, George Daws was ordered to be detained during Her Majesty's pleasure.

Camden

Nine-month-old William Theodore Sandys was suffering from diarrhoea and, on the advice of a surgeon, his mother sent a servant to the chemist to buy a pennyworth of antimonial wine.

Although he had been told countless times not to serve customers unless his master was present, sixteen-year-old apprentice Thomas Woodley prepared the mixture and labelled it. Throughout the morning, William was given three doses as directed, first fifteen drops, then twelve, then ten. However, the purpose of the wine was to make William vomit and, when he wasn't sick, his mother sent her maid back to the chemists to make sure this was right.

Chemists Mr Jones checked with Woodley and, to his horror, found that the apprentice had dispensed highly toxic wine of colchicum by mistake. Jones sent an emetic for William and asked surgeon Mr Harley to visit the baby as a matter of urgency, but

William died in the early hours of Christmas Day 1858. A post-mortem examination showed that the cause of his death was an overdose of colchicum.

At the subsequent inquest, held by deputy-coroner Mr Brent, the jury returned a verdict that 'the deceased died from the administration of colchicum wine instead of antimonial wine sold by Thomas Woodley and that blame attaches to his employer in permitting him to sell drugs in his absence.' Neither Jones nor Woodley appear to have faced any criminal charges in respect of William's death.

Mansion House

Thomas Forman appeared before the Lord Mayor of London at Mansion House on 22 December 1866, charged with attempting to cheat and defraud. On three occasions in the previous week, Forman presented himself at the offices of eminent bankers or solicitors, purporting to be delivering a Christmas hamper. Forman asked for 4s 10d for the carriage of the hamper from the station to the intended recipient. However, those receiving the hampers were invariably disappointed since they were filled with stones, with feathers, turkey and pheasants' feet, and hares' tails on the top to make them look authentic.

Mansion House. (Author's collection)

Forman's scam was terminated when one of his dupes realised that Forman didn't have the usual parcels delivery book with him. Forman said that his mate had it outside and that he would go and fetch it but solicitor's clerk Mr Hosgood smelled a rat and followed him, eventually carrying out a citizen's arrest when the 'mate' and delivery book could not be located.

Forman told the court that he had been out of work for a long time and he had a wife and four children to support. The Lord Mayor said he was 'a most impudent thief' and 'a rogue and a vagabond' and sentenced him to three months' hard labour in the House of Correction.

Bethnal Green

Eighty-year-old George Cecil was a former weaver, who fell on hard times in his old age and was forced to enter the Bethnal Green Workhouse.

On Christmas Day 1870, George was given permission to leave the Workhouse and have his lunch at his daughter's house. The permission was conditional on him returning to the Workhouse by five o'clock in the evening and, almost from the moment that he arrived at his daughter's house, George fretted about being late back. At twenty minutes to five, his anxiety reached fever pitch and he suddenly got up from his chair. 'I shall be too late,' he said, setting off at a run before anyone could stop him.

He knocked at the gatehouse door at about ten past the hour and breathlessly told gatekeeper Joseph Blinks, 'I'm late'.

'Never mind,' Blinks reassured him, only for George to drop down dead at his feet. A post-mortem examination later revealed that he had heart disease and that running and anxiety had caused his demise.

Chelsea

Several members of the Grenadier Guards stationed at Chelsea had been celebrating the festive season rather too enthusiastically and, on Christmas night 1876, four found themselves detained in the guardroom for drunkenness.

At about half-past eleven that night, Michael McConnon (or MacConnon) joined them, having returned to barracks very drunk. He was placed in the lock-up and, for a while, all was quiet until just after midnight, when the guards heard shouts of 'Murder!' When they went to investigate, they found twenty-seven-year-old Noah Johnson lying dead in a pool of blood and McConnon claiming to have killed him.

A post-mortem examination showed that Johnson had horrific injuries. He had cuts and bruises all over his body, his right ear was almost severed and he had three broken ribs, which had lacerated his liver, along with a build-up of blood between his skull and brain. Doctors were of the opinion that Johnson had been kicked to death and explained the fact that nobody had heard anything untoward by suggesting that the first kick would have rendered him unconscious.

McConnon was arrested by the civilian police and his boots, which were covered in clotted blood and hair, were taken from him. 'I don't care,' he responded when he was charged with Johnson's wilful murder

Twenty-five-year-old McConnon appeared before Mr Justice Hawkins at the Central Criminal Court on 11 January 1877. The court was told that there was absolutely no motive for Johnson's killing and that there was nothing to even suggest that he and McConnon had ever met before. McConnon, who was known to be quarrelsome and pugnacious when drunk, claimed to have absolutely no memory of anything between being in a beer shop with two friends and waking up in a cell, having been charged with Johnson's murder.

The jury took only five minutes to find him guilty and Hawkins sentenced him to death, telling him that there was not the slightest hope of a reprieve. However, on this occasion Hawkins was wrong and, just prior to his scheduled execution, McConnon's sentence was commuted to one of life imprisonment. Although the reason for this decision was not revealed, newspapers speculated that it was either due to the guards not having removed McConnon's boots before placing him in the cell or to the fact that Johnson had taken off his coat, suggesting that he may have fought his killer.

St George in the East

A few days before Christmas 1866, Maria Fuller asked her six-year-old daughter Margaret to keep her eye on her younger sister for a moment. Margaret was told that she was not to go beyond the street door but the lure of the brightly decorated shops proved irresistible and Margaret took her fifteen-month-old sister Emma to see them.

She didn't return for some time, by which time her mother was frantic with worry. Maria's anxiety increased when Emma began vomiting and gradually became more and more poorly as the day progressed.

Maria questioned Margaret about what had happened while she was out with her sister but it wasn't until evening that the little girl admitted to having fed Emma some 'white currants' that she found outside the greengrocer's shop. Having tasted a few of the currants herself and found them bitter, Margaret gave them to the baby.

Realising that Emma had probably been given mistletoe, Maria sent for Dr Spry, who prescribed an emetic. Emma vomited almost a teacup full of undigested berries but the surgeon's intervention came too late and, after a night spent screaming in agony, Emma died the next morning. A post-mortem examination showed that her stomach and intestines were highly inflamed from the actions of the mistletoe, which was an irritant poison.

At an inquest held by deputy coroner Mr Richards, it was agreed that Margaret could hardly be blamed for the tragedy and accordingly the inquest jury found that Emma was 'accidentally poisoned by mistletoe berries'.

Barnsbury

On Christmas Day 1868, a party was held at a house in Alfred Street, Barnsbury. There was dancing, good food and plenty of drink and everyone seemed to be having a wonderful time. In the evening, George Campbell suggested that a few of the men should retire upstairs for a tot of rum. Several took him up on the offer but as soon as they were upstairs, Campbell began to behave most strangely.

He first offered to wrestle, saying that he would bet 4s that he could throw anyone there. He then went to a cupboard and took out a rifle, which he began to play with. There was a paraffin lamp on the table and Campbell suddenly announced that he was going to put the light out. Before anyone could stop him, he pulled the trigger and John Moir fell to the ground dead, shot in the left temple.

A post-mortem examination showed that it was not a bullet that had killed Moir but the stopper fitted to the gun to protect it from dust and moisture when it was not in use. The stopper was in position when the gun was fired and had embedded itself in Moir's brain.

An inquest returned a verdict of wilful murder against Campbell, who was tried in January 1869. According to the prosecution, Campbell and Moir were great friends but Campbell felt that Moir had led him astray. Campbell was betrothed to a girl in his homeland of Scotland but, after a night out with Moir, the two young men got drunk and went off with a couple of young girls. Campbell seemed to feel that he had betrayed his sweetheart and talked dramatically of meeting her in heaven, saying that he had joined the army and was going to Bombay.

The rifle belonged to John Moir's brother, who insisted that it was not loaded and that the cartridges were kept in a separate room. Campbell's defence counsel made much of the fact that firing the gun with the stopper in could cause it to explode, thus Campbell was in great danger of injuring himself when he pulled the trigger. The stopper could also make the gun's aim inaccurate, in addition to which, Campbell had poor sight in his right eye. The defence maintained that Moir's death was a tragic accident, or at very worst, manslaughter rather than murder and the jury found him guilty of the lesser offence. In view of Campbell's previous good character, he was sentenced to twelve months' imprisonment.

Hampstead

On Christmas day 1870, the Rendell family of Hampstead were rudely awakened by the explosion of the boiler in their kitchen. When the smoke and steam cleared, the family's twenty-three-year-old cook Eliza Clarke was found dead, her body 'blown to atoms' by the force of the blast.

It was established that the cause of the explosion was a severe frost during Christmas Eve. When the boiler was lit on Christmas morning, the water was unable to circulate and pressure of the resulting steam, which had no means of venting, caused it to explode within fifteen minutes.

In recording a verdict of accidental death, the coroner recommended keeping the fire alight throughout the night during the winter months as a way of preventing such occurrences.

Tower Hamlets

Henry Armfield and William Spittle appeared before magistrates at the Thames Police Court on Christmas Eve 1878, charged with snowballing people in the street and with violently assaulting William Brown. Two days earlier, the men were among a crowd hanging around Canon Street Road, throwing snowballs at '…every respectable looking man or woman who passed.'

Those who dared to complain were either pushed or knocked down and on one occasion, a blow was struck that was hard enough to loosen three of the recipient's teeth. Magistrates found Armfield and Spittle guilty and sentenced them to one month's imprisonment with hard labour.

West Ham

Coroner Mr Lewis held an inquest at West Ham Hospital on Christmas Eve 1891 on the death of George Arthur Johnson.

Six-year-old George attended school in Stratford and on the previous day was given three slate pencils to take home and sharpen at lunchtime. George was very proud when he accomplished the task without any help and, on returning to school, rushed to show his teacher what a good job he had done. Unfortunately, he tripped and fell and one of the pencils stuck in his forehead.

George was taken to the nearest surgeon but the pencil could not be extricated so he was removed to West Ham Hospital, where he was anaesthetized and attempts were made to remove the pencil with forceps. It was so deeply embedded into the child's skull that it proved impossible to dislodge it and George died.

The cause of his death was given as asphyxia and the surgeons stated that the main problem was the administration of an anaesthetic so soon after he had eaten lunch. The inquest jury returned a verdict in accordance with the medical evidence

Hyde Park

By midday on Christmas Day 1835, several thousand people were enjoying themselves skating on The Serpentine in Hyde Park. Earlier that day, there had been several accidents and the Humane Society erected a number of boards bearing the word 'Dangerous' at various locations on the ice.

Suddenly, screams were heard coming from the north bank. Two male skaters had ventured into a dangerous area and were precipitated into the water when the ice broke beneath them. There was a rush to help them, putting excess weight onto the already fragile ice and before long there were several people floundering in the river.

Fifteen people were pulled out and taken to the Receiving House belonging to the Humane Society, where hot baths and other means of resuscitation were employed for upwards of two hours. Sadly, seven of those died.

Coroner Mr Higgs held an inquest at The Barley Mow public house on Grosvenor Square, at which the jury was expected to view the bodies of the seven victims, who were laid on the floor in a room at the inn. Many had fearful wounds on their chests and the jury was told that they were caused by the drag lines used to get them out of the water.

The key witnesses were members of the Humane Society, who stated that they had warned the skaters several times that they were in peril but were ignored. Asked why they did not rope off the dangerous areas, the Society explained that they had done so in the past but the skaters just cut the ropes and they could not afford to keep replacing them. When a juror suggested using chains, the Society pointed out the prohibitive cost and added that they believed that chains would be too heavy.

The inquest jury determined that the Humane Society had done all it reasonably could to preserve life and returned verdicts of 'accidental death' on all seven victims. On the same day, three more skaters drowned at St James's Park Lake.

Bethnal Green

The house at 9 Dixie Street, Bethnal Green, in one of the poorest areas of the East End, was occupied by two families. David Barber, his wife and child and his three sisters lived in two rooms on the ground floor, while the two upstairs rooms were tenanted by Mrs Sarah Jarvis and her nine children. Mr Jarvis normally lived there too but at Christmas 1897 he was in hospital suffering from consumption.

At half-past six on Boxing Day morning, Barber got up first and found his rooms full of smoke. He immediately woke his family and got them safely out of the house but his efforts to rouse the Jarvis family proved fruitless. The fire brigade were on the scene within two minutes but by then the whole house was well alight and the roof had collapsed.

Once the fire had been put out, firemen discovered the bodies of all ten members of the Jarvis family – Sarah (39), Hannah (16), Mary (14), Thomas (12), William (10), Louis (8), Alice (5), George (3), Caroline (2) and Elizabeth (8 months). Tragically, thirty-six-year-old John Jarvis also succumbed to his consumption that very day, the only bright side being that he died without ever knowing the fate of his entire family.

The bodies of all of the victims were completely charred and calcined and it was thought that the entire family had probably been overcome by smoke long before David Barber even discovered the existence of the fire. Mrs Jarvis was known as a respectable, temperate, hard working woman, who combined looking after her children with making matchboxes at home and although it proved impossible to determine the cause of the fire, it was suggested that one of the Jarvis family might have knocked over a lamp or a lighted candle. There was a large quantity of empty matchboxes in their rooms, ready to be collected after Christmas, which would have proved highly flammable.

The Barber family lost everything they owned, escaping from the fire almost naked. The contemporary newspapers were delighted to report that the spirit of Christmas abounded among their neighbours who, though poor, had done what they could to help.

London Bridge

On Christmas Day 1950, the Swedish cargo vessel *Rönnskär* was moored under London Bridge on the River Thames and Mrs Kathleen Holmer, the wife of the ship's Captain, Einer Holmer, was woken by her husband shaking her and telling her that the ship was on fire. The cabin was full of smoke and Holmer pushed his wife out through the window – she did not see her husband alive again.

When the blaze was finally extinguished, Holmer and Chief Engineer Sigvard Andersson were dead. Pathologist Dr Keith Simpson was later to confirm that both men were asphyxiated by the fumes from the fire.

London Bridge. (Author's collection)

Chief Officer Gustaf Agren told the inquest that he was shar-ing a cabin with Andersson and had tried to alert him after being awakened by smoke. Unable to rouse Andersson, Agren managed to escape by climbing through a porthole.

The police were satisfied that the fire was accidental and the inquest returned verdicts of 'accidental death' on both victims.

London

In 1854, many Londoners were forced to forego their Christmas dinners. People often relied on relatives in Scotland or Ireland to send them a turkey for Christmas, since they could be bought much cheaper there than in the City and, in an effort to evade duty, many of these turkeys were stuffed with bottles of whisky. 'All sorts of contrivances are adopted to defraud the revenue,' complained a contemporary newspaper.

However, at Christmas 1854, excise officers decided to crackdown on the practice and teams were employed at all of the major railway stations in the city. Any suspicious parcels were closely examined and, if the birds were found to contain contraband, they were impounded.

Bankside 🌿❦🌿

George Stephen Carter of Bermondsey got married in Southwark Cathedral on Christmas Day 1916. Immediately after the wedding, he and his new bride, Alice, went to her mother's home at Bankside, where they held what George would later describe as 'a honeymoon party'.

Having stayed overnight, the newlyweds prepared to leave for their marital home in Bermondsey on the evening of Boxing Day. Alice excused herself from the room momentarily to put on her hat and coat, and never returned.

After a frantic search revealed no trace of her, the police were notified of her disappearance. George and his mother-in-law both assured them that the bride was in excellent spirits, that she was perfectly sober and that there had been no quarrel before she seemingly vanished into thin air.

Alice's body was later recovered from the River Thames at Radcliff Cross, and, since nobody could work out how or why she ended up there, an inquest on her death returned an open verdict.

The jury were told that there was absolutely no suggestion that Alice would have committed suicide, which meant that her death was natural, an accident, or foul play. Alice's mother told the inquest that she saw her daughter go out through the front door without her hat and coat on and assumed that she was just going to say goodbye to one of the guests. Then, on 11 January 1917, a letter was received at Southwark police station. Dated 5 January, it read:

Sir – Regarding the missing woman Mrs George Stephen Carter, late of Noah's Ark Alley and married at Southwark Cathedral on December 25th 1916. I was on leave from France for Christmas and was in the named woman's company before and after her marriage. Knowing Bermondsey well, I spent a good part of my time around there. What has happened to Mrs Carter since I will not say in the letter – it is enough when I say I know all.

The letter was signed by someone purporting to be a Corporal in a Canadian Contingent and, although Alice's mother immediately

Southwark Cathedral. (Author's collection)

wrote to the address given, she received no reply. George Carter didn't recognise either the handwriting or the writer's name and address.

In concluding the inquest, the coroner said that he could think of absolutely no reason whatsoever why Mrs Carter should walk outside into a very cold, dark and foggy night without first putting on her hat and coat.

Kentish Town

Although not normally a drinker, twenty-seven-year-old John Joseph Crossman reluctantly allowed himself to be persuaded to have a drink at his mother-in-law's Christmas party. Sadly, on Christmas morning 1938, Crossman was found dead and a doctor attributed his death to acute alcoholic coma.

Joseph's brother, George, went with him to the party and told the subsequent inquest that people had goaded his brother into drinking. The normally temperate Joseph was given a double whisky, four brown ales and a pint of beer, and, in the words of coroner Mr W. Bentley Purchase, '. . . may have overestimated his capacity and drank more than was good for him.'

Bishopgate

Sixty-five-year-old Daniel Harte had only one leg and walked using crutches. Still, he was not about to let that fact ruin his enjoyment of the festive season and, on Christmas Eve 1862, he followed his usual tradition of 'drinking in' Christmas Day with a bottle of rum.

Having consumed a large quantity of neat spirits, Daniel disappeared from the family gathering on Christmas morning and it was assumed that he had gone to bed. However, when he did not appear for his Christmas dinner, a search of the house was made and Daniel was found dead on the floor of the coal cellar. He was covered with blood and his head was bent awkwardly underneath his body.

A doctor determined that he had died from suffocation and an inquest suggested that, in a drunken state, Harte had fallen into the coal cellar. Even if he were not rendered unconscious by the fall, having only one leg and being inebriated, he was unable to right himself and accidentally suffocated.

Kensington

Although she had separated from her husband three weeks earlier because of his violent behaviour towards her, Mary Alice Sexton was happy to grant her husband's request to see their son at Christmas. So, on Christmas Day 1930, she asked her sister to take James, who was almost three years old, round to her husband's home in Kensington.

Later, Mary and her sister went to fetch the child back for his Christmas dinner but when she knocked on the door of the house in St Mark's Road, she was met by abuse from her estranged husband and her mother-in-law. Suddenly, Charles Sexton ran back inside the house, returning seconds later with his hands dripping blood. 'That's beat you,' he said with satisfaction. 'You have neither got the boy now, nor have I.'

Charles had cut his son's throat with his father's razor and was charged at West London Police Court on Boxing Day with the wilful murder of James Robert Sexton. Charles, who was under summons from his wife for failing to maintain her and the boy, claimed that he was angry because Mary came to collect James only thirty minutes after dropping him off. Charles was later tried for his son's murder and found guilty but insane. He was ordered to be detained until His Majesty's pleasure be known.

New Malden

Sixty-year-old Samuel Jones of New Malden suffered from rheumatism and had been prescribed a lotion to rub into the affected parts of his body. The liquid, which was in a bottle that was clearly

marked 'Poison', was kept on his mantelshelf and Jones used it every day.

On Christmas morning 1884, Jones decided to treat himself to a glass of rum. His wife Ann heard him pouring liquid into a glass then immediately afterwards her husband said, 'Oh, Ann, I have taken the poison.' With that, he picked up the bottle of liniment and ran out of the house with a worried Ann behind him.

He went straight to his doctor's house and, having knocked on the door, told Dr Edwin Childs that he had drunk some of his medicine, which contained aconite and belladonna. Childs asked him how much he had taken and Jones replied, 'about ten drachms.' Childs immediately gave Jones an emetic and, when he didn't vomit within a few minutes, the doctor laid him on the floor and used a stomach pump to empty his stomach of its contents.

Jones was then allowed to go home but he became first drowsy then delirious and died at lunchtime. Since Jones had never shown any signs of wishing to commit suicide, an inquest determined that he had simply mistaken his lotion for rum and the jury returned a verdict of 'death from misadventure'.

St George in the East

On Christmas Day 1846, Mrs Dowdall of St George in the East cooked a leg of boiled pork for her family's dinner. As she was carving it at the table, her one-year-old daughter, Eliza, reached out and picked up a piece of meat, which she put in her mouth.

Within seconds, Eliza fell back in her chair lifeless. Thinking that her daughter was choking, Mrs Dowdall tried to clear her baby's mouth but was unable to do so. She rushed the baby to surgeon Mr Garrett but by the time she got there, Eliza was beyond medical assistance. A post-mortem examination showed that she had a piece of pork firmly lodged in her oesophagus, below the larynx.

At an inquest before coroner Mr Baker, the jury returned a verdict of 'accidental death'.

Islington

Lion tamer William Beaumont was performing at the World's Fair at the Agricultural Hall in Islington. On Christmas Eve 1895, one of the lions suddenly sprang at him, and clamped its teeth on his right arm.

Watched by hundreds of horrified spectators, the lion was driven back by Beaumont's assistants, giving him just enough time to get to his feet and make a dash for the cage's exit. He was taken to St Bartholomew's Hospital, where he was found to be suffering from a bite on his right arm and claw wounds on his thighs.

Initially, it seemed as though Beaumont would survive but he became delirious on Christmas Day, then began to show symptoms of hydrophobia. He died on 30 December.

Lewisham

In the early hours of the morning of Christmas Eve 1893, a child sleeping in a second-floor bedroom in Mercy Terrace, Lewisham was awakened by a crackling noise. He ran down to wake his mother, who was sleeping on the floor below and mother and son went downstairs together to investigate the strange sound. Once on the ground floor, they opened the back door of the house and the resulting draft immediately turned a hitherto small house fire into a raging inferno.

Flames raced up the stairwell, cutting off the most direct escape route of the nine people still upstairs. Fortunately, the fire brigade were quick to arrive but when they did, they found that all of the occupants had escaped by jumping from the first-floor windows.

Then, somebody realised that not everyone was safe. In the confusion, the residents congregated outside the house failed to notice that eight-year-old John Newnham was not amongst them. The fire brigade were informed and began to concentrate their hoses on John's second-floor bedroom to try and keep the fire in check, while a ladder was placed at the window. Two firemen ascended the ladder but found it 3 feet too short and had to go through a series of highly dangerous manoeuvres in order to gain entrance to the bedroom. Once inside, they found John huddled under his bed and carried him down to the ground. He was barely alive and died within minutes of being rescued.

The entire house was gutted by the fire and the occupants lost all of their possessions, none of which were insured. It proved impossible to determine the cause of the fire.

Note: Some sources state that the fire happened early on Christmas Day and not on Christmas Eve.

Edmonton

On Christmas Day 1866, Anne Gudgeon of Lower Edmonton complained of feeling unwell, saying that her head and throat felt bad. A surgeon was called to treat her but he could find nothing wrong, so recommended that she should put a mustard plaster on the back of her neck and rest. Anne went to bed at seven o'clock that evening but got up again four hours later and went downstairs, joining her husband and five children.

An hour later, the whole family went to bed. William Gudgeon noticed that his wife looked 'a little wild' and she complained that the light of his candle was hurting her eyes. William blew it out and was asleep within minutes.

He was awakened two hours later by his ten-year-old daughter, Selina, who claimed to have been woken by blood spurting onto her face. When she opened her eyes, she saw her mother crouching over her brother, Timothy George Gudgeon, clutching a razor. Four-year-old Tim's throat had been cut.

When Anne Gudgeon saw that Selina was awake, she caught hold of her. Terrified, Selina screamed and struggled, eventually sliding out of bed and running downstairs with her mother in pursuit. It was dark downstairs and Selina groped around until she felt a box of matches. When she struck one, the flame illuminated her mother in the act of cutting her own throat.

Selina raced upstairs to her father's room, where her nightmare continued. As she struggled to rouse her father, Selina saw her baby sister Elizabeth lying dead in their father's bed, her throat also cut.

It seems likely that Anne Gudgeon intended to murder her entire family and may well have succeeded had Selina not woken up. An inquest later returned a verdict of wilful murder against Anne in respect of the deaths of the two children, attributing Anne's own death to suicide while in a state of temporary insanity.

Whitechapel

Between two and three o'clock on the morning of Christmas Day 1860, a passing policeman noticed smoke coming from the premises of cabinet maker Mr Hopps. He raised the alarm, managing to wake Mr Hopps and his wife and daughter and their lodgers, Mr and Mrs Hibbet, and sending for the fire brigade and the portable fire escape.

The Hibbets, Mr and Mrs Hopps and one of their children managed to climb down a ladder to safety from the first floor. However, there were still three of the Hopps children in a back bedroom.

The portable fire escape was placed up against the burning building and someone began to climb it with the intention of entering the house through an upstairs window and searching for the children. Just then, someone broke open the street door and the flames suddenly roared up through the house, thwarting any attempts to enter.

Mr and Mrs Hopps were frantic and had to be held back to prevent them from running into the inferno. As soon as the fire was under control, two firemen bravely went into the burning building to search for the children but they were too late – twelve-year-old Sarah, eight-year-old Elizabeth and six-year-old Henry were burned to a cinder.

Clerkenwell

Fifty-five-year-old Dinah Weeden of Clerkenwell was very fond of rum, even keeping a bottle in her bedroom so that she could have a swig during the night. On Christmas Eve 1892, Dinah drank more rum than usual and, on Christmas morning, she was found lying dead on her bed.

A doctor was summoned and found that the inside of the dead woman's mouth was burned, as if she had drunk something corrosive. On a table in Dinah's room was a bottle of carbolic acid, which was used as a disinfectant, and, although the bottle was clearly labelled, the liquid it contained was reddish-brown in colour and bore more than a passing resemblance to rum.

A post-mortem examination confirmed the doctor's initial suspicions that death was due to carbolic acid poisoning and, at a later inquest, coroner Dr Wynn Westcott determined that, since there was no reason to suggest that Dinah had any thoughts of suicide, she must have accidentally mistaken the carbolic acid for rum. The jury returned a verdict of 'death from misadventure'.

St Pancras

At about eight o'clock in the evening of Christmas Day 1869, a multi-tenanted house in Sandwich Street caught fire. An old lady who lived on the second floor heard a crackling noise in the room next door and brought it to the attention of landlord John Winnett, who went to check and found a fire blazing. Winnett raised the alarm and, with the aid of his family and a neighbour, began to remove his furniture from the premises.

He was well aware that a family named Beetlestone lived on the top storey but later maintained that the staircase was on fire and it was impossible to reach them

The house was only a matter of yards from the fire station and the locations of more than one portable fire escape, which were on the scene within twenty minutes. Even so, everyone on the third floor of the building perished in the conflagration.

Thirty-year-old Mary Ann Beetlestone had only given birth four days earlier and she and her infant son died along with her other children, Francis (10), Alice (5) and Frank (2), as well as a neighbour, Rosina Brown (8), who was visiting the family when the fire broke out.

At an inquest on the six deaths held by coroner Dr Lankester, the jury were told that the fire brigade had attended promptly and the portable fire escapes were quickly deployed, although there was a problem with one of them, which caught fire. The jury found that the deceased persons died from suffocation, at a fire arising from accidental causes. They asked the coroner to strongly censure John Winnett, who left the door of the room open when he first discovered the fire, facilitating its spread through the house. They were also disgusted by the fact that he tried to save his own furniture, knowing that there was a family on the third floor and that the only adult would be incapacitated, having so recently given birth. Not only that but inexplicably, Winnett also failed to alert the police, fire brigade or his neighbours to the fact that that the Beetlestone family were still in the building.

Wandsworth

Nine-year-old William Henry Stannard and his thirteen-year-old brother Frederick were playing together at their home in Twilly Street, Wandsworth, on Christmas Eve 1920.

Frederick picked up a saloon rifle belonging to their father that he had found in the parlour. 'If a Sinn Feiner comes in, I'll make him put his hands up,' he announced.

William walked out of the room and, when he came back, Frederick raised the rifle to his shoulder and pulled the trigger. Unfortunately, the gun was loaded and William was shot in the chest, dying soon afterwards.

'Without wanting to say severe things against the parents, one could not help feeling how regrettable it was that anything in the way of cartridges should be left where children could get at them,' remarked coroner Mr Ingleby Oddie as he recorded the inquest jury's verdict of 'accidental death'.

Chelsea

Twenty-three-year-old Alfred Wood had been courting Alice for some months when, on Christmas Day 1914, a soldier unexpectedly turned up on the doorstep of the house in Chelsea, where she lived with her two sisters and a brother-in-law. When Albert Dickinson returned from India, his first thought was to visit his girlfriend Alice and he was completely unprepared to find Wood there. Wood was equally surprised and shocked to learn of Dickinson's existence and the two men fought.

Unfortunately Wood died, but a post-mortem examination revealed that the cause of his death was not violence but an aneurism of the brain, which could easily have burst at any time, especially if he became 'excited'.

It was left to an inquest jury to determine whether Wood's death could be blamed on Dickinson, who, it was alleged, had not only kicked Wood as he lay unconscious on the ground but had also picked him up and hit him in the face.

When Dickinson insisted that he had only struck Wood in self-defence and denied having kicked him at all, the inquest jury returned a verdict of 'death from natural causes'.

Perrivale

Mark Mason Ezart was walking home to Shepherd's Bush on Christmas Eve 1932 when a trench dug in the pavement forced him into the gutter.

Van driver John James Hammerton was driving the same route, when he was suddenly dazzled by the headlights of a vehicle coming in the opposite direction. Hammerton pulled into the side of the road to allow the oncoming vehicle to pass but unfortunately collided with Ezart, who was walking with his back to the traffic and wearing dark clothing.

Ezart died at the scene of the accident. He was to have been married on Christmas Day.

An inquest jury returned a verdict of 'accidental death', exonerating Hammerton from any blame for the fatality.

Bloomsbury

Two-year-old Alice Stanford had been a patient at Great Ormond Street Hospital for Sick Children for some time, suffering from what doctors described as 'chronic disease'. On Christmas Day 1875, nurse Elizabeth Williams took Alice for a bath.

Great Ormond Street Hospital. (Author's collection)

She ran the bathwater and tested it, finding it tepid and, since Alice was known to dislike water, took no notice when the toddler screamed as she was lowered into the bath. Elizabeth then left Alice for a few moments while she collected a towel from the ward and, when she returned, she discovered that Alice was badly scalded.

Alice died from shock on Boxing Day as a direct result of her scalds and, at the inquest on her death, Nurse Williams stated that she could not recall whether or not the hot tap was still running when she put the child in the bath. Matron Mrs Hay told the inquest that Nurse Williams was a kind, cheerful girl and stated that no accident of this kind had ever happened at the hospital before.

The inquest jury debated the matter for a long time before returning a verdict of 'death by misadventure' and requesting the coroner to caution Nurse Williams about her future conduct.

Islington

On Christmas Eve 1912, railwaymen on their way to work spotted a fire in Copenhagen Street, Islington. The house was located less than 200 yards from the local fire station, so the fire brigade reached the blaze very quickly. However, the fire spread rapidly through the three-storey house, the staircase acting like a chimney.

It was impossible to use the stairs as an escape route. The house was lived in by three families, each of which occupied a separate floor. The Colembeck family on the ground floor managed to walk out through the door, while the Moore family on the first floor were rescued through the windows by firemen using ladders.

Sadly, members of the Score family perished in their rooms on the second floor. Fifty-year-old Alfred Score was seen briefly leaning out of the window of his bedroom, when some of his neighbours urged him to jump and others shouted at him to stay put. By the time the portable fire escape was placed in position, Alfred had disappeared and firemen were unable to find him or and of his family, apart from twenty-year-old Ada Score. When the fire was finally extinguished, Alfred's body and that of his wife and two of his daughters were removed from the ashes. Alfred and Susan Score had both died from burns, while their daughters Hilda and Ethel had suffocated.

Ada was badly burned on her arms, face and body and was taken to the Royal Free Hospital, where her condition was described as 'critical'. She had one other sister, who had chosen to stay with her grandparents that night and thus escaped the tragedy that destroyed almost her entire family in a matter of minutes.

King's Cross Station

On Christmas Day 1889, brothers-in-law Herman Rohl and Carl Karropowski were travelling together by train to visit relatives near Farringdon Street. Just after King's Cross Station, Rohl wanted some fresh air and so opened the window of the carriage in which they were travelling and stuck his head out. No sooner had he done so than he fell back into the carriage bleeding from a terrible wound in his head.

He appeared to be quite dead and when the train stopped at Farringdon Street, he was taken to hospital, where life was pronounced extinct. Coroner Mr Langham held an inquest on his death and the jury heard that a railway employee was climbing onto a train on the adjacent rail when thirty-three-year-old Rohl's head collided with the open door. The jury returned a verdict of 'accidental death'.

Islington

A grand Christmas pageant was staged at the Agricultural Hall, Islington on the theme of 'Meeting of the Monarchs'. On Christmas Eve 1866, almost 20,000 spectators attended and after the pageant had circled the arena twice, the crowd were still shouting for more, so it was decided to send the procession round for a third circuit.

One of the floats was 30 feet high and weighed nearly five tons. It was a representation of 'The Queen of England and her Court' and was pulled by a matched team of nine cream-coloured horses. Each of the horses was led by a groom dressed in the Royal livery and, as the float reached the western end of the arena, one of the

Agricultural Hall, Islington, 1909. (Author's collection)

grooms stumbled and fell. Before the float could be stopped it rolled over him and Thomas Gibson was crushed to death.

A post-mortem examination showed that Gibson's injuries were not as severe as might have been expected. He had a broken thigh and three broken ribs, along with some slight bruising and minor abrasions, but, according to surgeon Mr Butler, none of his injuries were fatal. Butler found that Gibson's brain was very congested and theorised that the exertion of going round and round the arena had caused the deceased to become giddy and this giddiness, combined with the injuries, produced a state of syncope (fainting), resulting in death.

Pimlico

As a policeman was patrolling his beat in Alderney Street, Pimlico on Christmas Eve 1928, he saw a little girl running down the middle of the road, enveloped in a ball of flames. The policeman gave chase, eventually catching the child and enveloping her in his coat.

Twelve-year-old Renee Wineberg was taken by ambulance to St George's Hospital, where she died on Boxing Day from severe burns. An inquest was held by coroner Mr Ingleby Oddie, at which it was revealed that Rene was decorating a Christmas tree when her nightdress accidentally came into contact with a coal fire and burst into flames, after which she ran into the street in a state of panic.

The inquest jury returned a verdict of 'accidental death'.

Southwark

On Christmas Eve 1898, Mrs Taylor of Dock Head and her nine-month-old daughter were both very poorly. Mr Taylor had to go out to work and so left his wife and daughter in bed, making sure that everything they might need while he was out was on the bedside table, within easy each.

That afternoon, Mrs Taylor gave baby Violet Mary Kate a dose of medicine. She realised almost immediately that she had made a dreadful mistake and given the child a fatal dose of carbolic acid but sadly the realisation came too late for Violet, who died soon afterwards.

Coroner Mr S.F. Langham held an inquest at Guy's Hospital, at which Mr Taylor gave evidence that the child's medicine and the carbolic acid were in almost identical bottles, containing what looked like identical liquids. He explained that it was vital for the two bottles to be together on the bedside table, since Mrs Taylor was unable to get out of bed.

'My wife's brain is now in the balance,' Taylor told the jury, begging them not to add any rider to their verdict that would blame her for their daughter's death. 'Please don't kill her with such a decision,' he implored them.

'Our verdict is one of death by misadventure, with a rider that no blame is due to anyone,' the foreman of the jury reassured him.

North Kensington

Three-year-old Lilian Mary Morris woke at three o'clock on Christmas morning 1924 and was ecstatic to discover that Father Christmas had visited and filled her stocking with toys. As she ran around her grandmother's house excitedly showing the contents of her stocking to her relations, her flannelette nightgown accidentally brushed against a lighted candle and burst into flames. Lilian suffered terrible burns all over her body and died from the effects on Boxing Day. An inquest held at Paddington later recorded a verdict of 'accidental death'.

Bloomsbury

Twenty-seven-year-old Clara Boswell (aka Burton, Buswell and Harriet Boswell) supplemented her income as a member of the *corps de ballet* on the London stage with prostitution. On Christmas Eve 1891, she returned to her lodgings in Great Coram Street and gave her landlady Harriet Wright half a sovereign for her rent, receiving a shilling change.

She went to her room with a man, who was heard to leave the house early on Christmas morning. When no further movement was heard from Clara's room, the other occupants of the house forced an entry that afternoon. They found Clara lying dead on her bed, a stab wound under her left ear and her throat cut. The shilling from her landlady was missing, as were her earrings and a few other trinkets.

The police spoke to witnesses who had seen and spoken to Clara on Christmas Eve and found that her male companion was a foreigner, probably a German. He was described as 'about twenty-five years of age, 5ft 9in tall, with neither beard, whiskers nor moustache but not having shaved for two or three days, his beard when grown would be rather dark. He has a swarthy complexion and blotches or pimples on his face …'

Some people confessed to the murder and arrests were made, but the true identity of the killer eluded the police until they heard that a German brig, *Wangerland*, had been under repair at Ramsgate at the time of the murder and that a member of the crew closely fitted the description of Clara's escort. Police held an identity parade and witnesses positively identified ship's chaplain Dr Henry James Bernhard Gottfried Hessel as the man with Clara on the night of her death. Hessel, who had volunteered to be a part of the parade to make up the numbers, found himself arrested and gaoled pending a hearing before magistrates.

Several people were positive that Hessel was Clara's companion and therefore her murderer, but when he appeared before magistrates it quickly became evident that he had an unshakeable alibi for 24, 25 and 26 December and he was discharged. The police were heavily criticised for not checking his alibi and subjecting an innocent man to twelve days' imprisonment, although it later emerged that Hessel was known as a drunkard, who was suspected of misappropriating Church funds to feed his habit. Nevertheless, he did not seem to be a killer and the murder of Clara Boswell went unsolved.

Clerkenwell

Mrs Jane Pettingall (Pettingell/Pettengill) was at home in Clerkenwell on 27 December 1878 when she happened to glance over at the table. There were three glasses on it, each containing some leftover beer and, Mrs Pettingall's thirteen-year-old step-daughter, Elizabeth Ann, was surreptitiously pouring some liquid from a bottle into one of them, leaving the room as soon as she had finished what she was doing.

The bottle contained phosphor paste, used for killing rats and mice. When questioned, Elizabeth freely admitted that she had intended to poison her stepmother and that she had given her eight-year-old sister, Emma, a penny to buy the poison for her.

Elizabeth was brought before magistrates charged with an unlawful attempt to administer poison, so as to endanger life. 'It is quite true. I did intend to poison her,' she told magistrates calmly.

Her father, Thomas, testified that Elizabeth was completely out of his control. Her former employer had accused her of theft but refused to press charges because of her age. Thomas said that he had personally handed her in to the police, after his wife complained that the child tried to poison her. When ques-tioned, Elizabeth said that she wanted to kill her stepmother simply because she didn't like her – there had been no quarrel between them.

Elizabeth was tried at the Middlesex Sessions, held at the Central Criminal Court on 13 January 1879, where she was found guilty. Because of her age, it was difficult to decide how best to punish her and the judgement was deferred until the February Sessions. There Elizabeth was sentenced to six weeks' imprisonment at Newgate Prison, to run from 13 January, after

The condemned cell in Newgate.

which she was to go to a reformatory for three years. She appears to have served her time in the Northamptonshire Reformatory for Girls.

Woolwich

On Christmas Eve 1899, Mrs Hayden of Gough Yard, Woolwich went out for a drink with a female friend, leaving her two children at home alone. As far as Mrs Hayden was concerned, four-year-old Thomas and two-year-old Charlotte were sleeping soundly and were unlikely to wake up and so she could see no harm in slipping out for an hour or two of fun.

When she returned home, there were fire engines outside. Neighbours had seen smoke billowing from her house and tried to get in, but were beaten back by smoke and flames. Eventually, someone smashed a window and was able to climb through it and rescue the children but, although they were rushed straight to a doctor, both were dead from burns and the effects of smoke inhalation.

Deputy coroner Mr Wood told Mrs Hayden that she had no business going out and leaving such young children in a room with a fire in it. The jury agreed but although they asked the coroner to censure the children's parents, they fell short of recommending any criminal charges when they returned verdicts of 'accidental death' on both children.

Islington

'I think there has been a bit of a murder done in my shop,' said the man who approached PC Cooke on Christmas night 1916. 'Will you come round? My son has done it out of revenge.'

Cooke found thirty-year-old William Andrew Leach dead on the floor of the shop from a single stab wound in his chest. Leach's nephew, twenty-one-year-old Frederick William Leach, readily claimed responsibility. 'I did it out of revenge as he broke my mother's nose,' he explained.

Leach was a Private in the Oxford and Bucks Light Infantry, who had seen action in France during the First World War. He was obviously drunk and, as he was escorted to the police station, he claimed to be seeing Germans and suggested outflanking them.

An inquest heard that Frederick had been drunk for most of Christmas Day, as had his whole family, and an argument over Christmas dinner ended with him stabbing his uncle. The inquest jury returned a verdict of wilful murder against him and he appeared before Mr Justice Darling at the Central Criminal Court.

Darling was impressed that Frederick Leach had joined the army early instead of waiting to be called-up and that he was an exemplary soldier. When the jury found Leach guilty of the lesser charge of manslaughter, Darling blamed the offence on drink and the fact that Leach's whole family spent Christmas Day in '. . . a most discreditable manner.' He sentenced Leach to eighteen months' imprisonment with hard labour.

Mr Justice Darling. (Author's collection)

Westminster

Sixty-three-year-old Henry Gillett of Great Peter Street, Westminster had 'given himself up to drink.' Whenever he was drunk – which he frequently was – he would beat his wife Margaret.

Between nine and ten o'clock at night on Christmas Day 1875, Henry came home intoxicated and demanded money from his long-suffering wife. When she wouldn't give him any, he punched and kicked her and tore handfuls of her hair out by the roots. Margaret pleaded with him to go to bed quietly but he continued to abuse her, eventually kicking her down a flight of stairs.

Terrified for her life, Margaret fled, eventually staying the night with a neighbour. When she returned home on Boxing Day, she found her husband lying dead on the floor and a post-mortem examination showed that the cause of his death was apoplexy, aggravated by his heavy drinking.

EASTERN

When Mrs Jane Palmer went to visit her daughter on the morning of Christmas Eve 1900, she was shocked to find her cottage door open and to hear groans coming from within. Mrs Palmer found twenty-seven-year-old widow Thirza Kelly of Stokesby, Norfolk lying on her bed, having been stabbed seven times in the abdomen. (Thankfully, her fourteen-week-old baby lay beside her unharmed.)

The police and a doctor were called and, since Thirza was so badly injured, a magistrate was also brought to her bedside, in the hope that she would make a deposition. Unfortunately, she died before this could be done but she had already given police the name of her assailant.

Acting on her information, the police arrested seventeen-year-old John Edward Cossey, who lived about 300 yards from Mrs Kelly. Cossey admitted to being attracted to the young widow and to breaking into her house through a back window after a night of drinking. When he burst into Thirza's bedroom, she screamed and fought him and so he stabbed her to shut her up.

An inquest returned a verdict of wilful murder against Cossey and the coroner censured the dead woman's next-door neighbour, who testified to hearing a woman and baby screaming for ten minutes. James Gowen looked out of his bedroom window and, seeing nothing untoward, went back to bed leaving his neighbour to her grisly fate.

Although only seventeen, Cossey had a history of strange behaviour. He had once stolen women's underclothing from his employer and dressed himself in it while he slaughtered a pig, before hanging up the carcass and stuffing the underwear inside it. At his trial, Dr Thompson of the Norfolk Lunatic Asylum suggested that Cossey suffered from a kind of perversion, which led to him taking pleasure from bloodshed and killing. Nevertheless, the jury found Cossey guilty and he was sentenced to death, although a recommendation was made for mercy on account of his youth.

Cossey was eventually reprieved, although it is not known whether this was due to concerns about his mental state or his age at the time of Mrs Kelly's murder. He was sent to Chelmsford Prison.

Chelmsford Prison, 1906. (Author's collection)

Ipswich

On Christmas Day 1900, John Kent went out at nine o'clock in the morning, leaving his wife, sixty-three-year-old Elizabeth, preparing the Christmas dinner. The couple's son left home an hour after his father, telling his mother that he would not be back until that evening.

At just after midday, Elizabeth spoke to a neighbour while they were both out in their yards but when her husband got back at two o'clock, there was no sign of her, or of dinner.

John Kent searched the bedrooms and the back yard and, when he couldn't find his wife, he assumed that she had gone out and sat down for a snooze. As the evening approached and Elizabeth Kent was still unaccountably absent, her husband finally thought to check the cellar, where he found her unconscious at the foot of the steps.

Kent carried his wife upstairs and laid her carefully on the sofa but, since she wasn't bleeding, he didn't think she was badly hurt and so didn't send for a doctor. It wasn't until a neighbour dropped in later that evening and advised him to seek medical attention that he was finally galvanised into action.

Surgeon Mr J.R. Staddon arrived at nine o'clock in the evening and told Kent that he believed that Mrs Kent had a fractured skull. Staddon left directions for her care and called back the following morning, when Mrs Kent was still unconscious.

Elizabeth Kent died on 27 December and Staddon stated at the inquest that she died from compression of the brain caused by haemorrhage from the fracture at the base of her skull. Under questioning by the coroner, Staddon said that he didn't believe he could have saved the deceased if he had been called out earlier. The inquest was told that Elizabeth was perfectly sober but that she was known to suffer from dizzy spells on occasions and the jury returned a verdict in accordance with the medical evidence.

Arlesey

In 1876, the Great Northern Railway ran on the 'absolute block system' – each section or block of the track was controlled by a signalman, who 'offered' each train to the next signalman down the line. If the line was clear, that signalman 'accepted' the train.

The system went wrong on 23 December, when a luggage train at Arlesey Siding Station in Bedfordshire was allowed to shunt across the down line. Unfortunately it derailed and, since there was not enough time to relay the information about the blocked line to the signalmen, the Manchester express train barrelled into it at full speed.

When the dust settled, the six carriages pulled by the express train were seen to be completely smashed. The Three Counties

Asylum was very near to the station and, within minutes, medical staff arrived to help the injured and dying.

The bodies of driver Thomas Pepper and stoker George Smith were picked up about 100 yards from the crash. They had obviously realised the inevitability of a collision and tried to jump clear of the train but were killed by the fall. Passengers Abigail (or Helen) Longstaff, Lucy Thompson and Maurice Michael were also killed, while the stationmaster was said to have temporarily lost his reason. A large number of passengers were injured but a surprising number walked away from the devastating crash unscathed.

Pepper was a highly experienced driver, who had won bonuses for careful driving and there was argument about whether he had ignored the danger signals or if they had not been set. An inquest and an official inquiry suggested that Pepper simply didn't see the signals in sufficient time to stop. He was aware that there was another express train minutes behind him and, given the weight and speed of his own train and the slipperiness of the rails due to the weather conditions, he did not have sufficient brake power or stopping distance.

Barking

Mr Ager of Barking, Essex, was playing cards with his two sons, Percy and eighteen-year-old Clifford, at a family party on Christmas Day. Earlier in the evening, Clifford and Percy had dressed up and performed a little skit to amuse the guests and Percy's nine-year-old son George decided that it would be good fun to do something similar. Unnoticed by the adults, he left the room, returning minutes later wearing his Scout hat and his uncle's coat.

'Hands up, Uncle Clifford,' George demanded as he pulled a pistol from the coat pocket and fired. The bullet hit Clifford on the temple and he died soon afterwards.

The inquest heard that Clifford had a lifelong fascination with firearms and had frequently bought guns in the past, which his mother usually took from him and threw in the river. He was due to join the Air Force after Christmas and was very much looking forward to it. Young George was a great fan of the Wild West and had read books that taught him that a good cowboy was always quick on the draw.

Coroner Dr Ambrose recorded a verdict of 'accidental death' at the subsequent inquest, describing Clifford's habit of carrying a loaded pistol in his overcoat pocket as 'almost criminal negligence' that had led to the loss of the life of a fine young man and most probably mentally scarred a child for the rest of his days.

Bedingfield

On Christmas Day 1861, thirty-three-year-old John Flatt went to see a friend at Mr Cracknell's mill at Bedingfield, Suffolk. As he left, he inadvertently stepped within range of the windmill's revolving sails, which hit him hard on the head.

Although nobody actually saw the accident happen, workmen heard a loud thumping noise and found Flatt lying insensible in a pool of blood. He was found to have a broken nose, a contused wound on his right temple and his front teeth were loosened, and, although a doctor was called, he died from his injuries the next morning.

Coroner Mr F.B. Marriott held an inquest at Rishangles the following day, at which it was stated that the mill was not going at full speed at the time of the accident and that the sails passed within 4 feet of the ground. The jury returned a verdict of 'accidental death'.

Thetford

When the 2.05 p.m. train from Shoreditch failed to arrive at Norwich Station on Christmas Eve 1845, it was assumed that the delay was caused by extra traffic on the line due to the season. However, when the mail train also failed to arrive at 6.55 p.m. it was obvious that there had been some sort of catastrophe, which turned out to be the derailment at Thetford of the first train. Having left the rails, the engine dragged all the carriages with it, skidding for some 50 yards before falling over an embankment and landing on its side.

The train driver, William Pickering, was almost decapitated while the stoker, Richard Hedger (or Hedges), was terribly injured. One of his legs was cut off and the other mangled and, having been extricated from the wreckage with difficulty, he survived only a few hours. By a miracle, none of the passengers were hurt, other than suffering from shock and minor cuts and bruises. Most were able to walk to Thetford Station after the crash.

An inquest was opened into the two deaths, at which it was established that, at the time of the crash, Pickering was driving far too fast and had been signalled to slow down since that area of track had recently been repaired. According to the platelayer who was engaged in repairing the line when Pickering's train passed, he took no heed of the 'slow down' signal but just shook his head and continued travelling at more than sixty miles per hour.

The inquest jury were divided, with twelve wishing to return verdicts of 'accidental death caused by the imprudent conduct of the engine driver in going at an excessive speed', while the remaining three jurors had concerns about the design of the train itself and held out for 'accidental death caused by the misconduct of the engine driver and the defective construction of the engine'. The coroner took the majority verdict.

Bury St Edmunds

Two men were out walking with a dog on Christmas morning 1900, when the animal found a brown paper-wrapped parcel in a hedgerow at Bury St Edmunds, Suffolk. The dog began worrying the package and, when the men went to see what was exciting it so, they found that the parcel contained the dead body of a baby girl.

Dr Charles Scott Kilner examined the body, finding it to be that of a full term, newly born baby. There was a collection of blood between the baby's scalp and skull and a closer investigation revealed that the skull was fractured above the bridge of the infant's nose. The fracture extended across the child's forehead to the top of her right eye socket and there were also fractures of the left and right parietal bones, at the side of the skull. Kilner believed that the baby had been murdered and that considerable force was used, with at least two blows to the head.

The inquest jury returned a verdict of 'wilful murder by person or person's unknown'.

Great Waltham

In the village of Great Waltham, Essex, a group of musicians and carol singers were proceeding from house to house on Christmas Eve 1842. At most homes, their performance was rewarded with alcohol and the party quickly became quite quarrelsome.

At first, there was a bit of pushing and shoving. Frederick Olive pushed John Wood so hard that he fell over and then Olive had a brief fight with a man named Brown. Elijah Olive and John Wood had a short skirmish but Wood walked away after Elijah hit him in the mouth. Frederick Olive then pushed William Bush down and John Gowers hit Frederick, who fell over. When he stood up, Gowers hit him a second time and this time Frederick didn't get up.

His twin brother, Elijah, told him to stop sulking but twenty-one-year-old Frederick insisted that he couldn't get up and that Gowers had blinded him. He was hauled to his feet and propped against a wall and later taken into The Six Bells public house, where he died. An inquest returned a verdict of manslaughter against Gowers, who was committed for trial on the coroner's warrant.

He appeared at the Essex Assizes in March 1843 and, once he had pleaded not guilty, the counsel for the defence stated that

Great Waltham, 1905. (Author's collection)

he had evidence to show that Olive's death was caused by other circumstances that had nothing to do with any blow struck by his client. After a brief discussion with the counsel for the prosecution, the latter informed the judge that he didn't intend to offer any evidence against Gowers, who was promptly discharged.

Godmanchester

In 1852, nineteen-year-old Eliza Legge went to spend Christmas with her mother and grandmother at Godmanchester, Cambridgeshire. At two o'clock on Christmas morning, the roof of the house suddenly fell in, crushing Eliza beneath at least five hundredweight of tiles, joists and rafters and killing her instantly. Her grandmother, with whom she was sharing a room, was lucky to escape with severe bruising.

The cottage was built only twelve years earlier but had been improperly constructed. Water seeped through the roof tiles, soaking the rafters and rotting them to the point where they were unable to support the roof. The poor state of the timbers had been spotted six months earlier when some repairs were carried out and, although it was pointed out that the roof was in a dangerous state, nothing was done to rectify it.

Godmanchester, 1904. (Author's collection)

Friday Bridge, near Wisbech

On Christmas Eve 1873, a group of around twenty people travelling by rail from Peterborough to Wisbech were accidentally left at Peterborough Station. They managed to get as far as March on the mail train then, after waiting at the station there for more than an hour, they were told that there were no further trains to Wisbech.

After a discussion, twelve of the group decided to walk to their various destinations. However, it was a very dark night and they had difficulty finding their way.

At one point on their journey, their road skirted an artificial drainage ditch known as the Twenty Foot or Twenty Feet River and somehow sixty-three-year-old John Ireland walked off the bank into the water. The Northamptonshire farmer shouted for help and the party gathered on the bank, helpless to do anything to save him since not one of them could swim. Eventually, Ireland's eighteen-year-old son could stand his father's plaintive cries no longer and even though he was unable to swim, he threw himself into the water fully clothed and immediately sank without a trace.

The two bodies were recovered at daybreak on Christmas Day and a later inquest recorded verdicts of 'accidentally drowned' on both father and son.

Ilford

On 22 December 1933, Sydney Alfred Baker of Ilford, Essex, bought some fried fish for himself, his heavily pregnant wife and their two children, four-year-old Betty and two-year-old Bernard. On tasting the fish, Baker felt that it was a little undercooked but he was so hungry that he ate it anyway.

The whole family fell ill and spent a wretched Christmas with stomach pains and sickness. Then, on Boxing Day, there was a knock on the door. Baker opened it and was promptly arrested by the police for being in arrears with his rates. In spite of his protests that his wife and children were ill, Baker was taken to Brixton Prison. Meanwhile, the children's condition worsened and both were taken to East Ham hospital.

When the Governor of Brixton
Prison was informed on 31
December that Baker's children
were critically ill, he immedi-

ately paid his outstanding debt out of his own pocket and released
him. Baker rushed to the hospital but sadly his son and daughter
had died before he got there.

Post-mortem examinations showed that both children were
infected with an organism similar to typhoid, which was known
to result from eating infected and improperly cooked fish. The
coroner did not blame the vendor, Mr Samuels, since it was highly
possible that the fish were contaminated when he bought them.
However, he did feel it inappropriate to arrest a father with young
children on Boxing Day, particularly since the warrant for Baker's
arrest was issued in November.

The coroner strongly censured the local police for leaving a
heavily pregnant woman, who was unwell, alone in charge of two
very poorly children. 'The Christmas message seems to have been
entirely lost,' he concluded.

Hatfield

The train to Peterborough left King's Cross Station on Boxing
Day 1870 at 4.25 p.m. Near Hatfield, Hertfordshire, the engine
driver felt that something was amiss and, looking back, he
realised that the train had broken free of its couplings. He
walked back down the line and met the train's guard, who told
him that the train had derailed and asked him to drive on to
Hatfield for help.

It seems as if one of the wheels on the brake van had been
weakened by frost and shattered into several pieces, causing the
van and two following carriages to overturn. George Blake,
Thomas P. Reynolds, Harry Rawlings, James Pullen, George
Augustus Potter and Thomas Bransom were killed, as were Mrs
Oswin and Mrs Kershaw.

The two women were the wife and sister of a signalman,
who just happened to be walking along the line to take him his
evening meal when the brake van fell on them.

Norwich

Nineteen-year-old Horace Alfred Cox and twenty-year-old Alice Parker had been courting for ten months and were planning to get married. Every Tuesday and Friday night, they would go for walks together and on Tuesday, 23 December 1898, Horace asked Alice if she would spend Christmas Day with him at his parents' house in South Heigham.

Alice told him that she was very sorry but she had to work on Christmas Day at the café in St Benedict's Street, Norwich, where she was employed. Horace seemed terribly disappointed and on Christmas Eve he twice visited the café to see if Alice had changed her mind. Patiently, Alice explained that she had to work and couldn't possibly get away and, on Horace's second visit, with

no warning, he suddenly pulled a revolver out of his pocket, aimed it at her and fired.

Fortunately for Alice, she was walking through a swinging door at the time. The glass in the door deflected the bullet, which passed through the collar of her dress, scorching her neck.

Alice shrieked and ran for the door which led to the café's stairs. Horace followed and, when the proprietor of the café appeared to see what all the commotion was about, Horace fired at him too, again shooting wide of his target. He shot at Alice a second time and missed before placing the gun against his own head and pulling the trigger, blowing his brains out.

It was said at the inquest that Horace had been in a despondent frame of mind for some time and that he was very jealous, although Alice insisted that she had never given him the slightest reason to feel that way. The inquest jury returned a verdict that Cox had committed suicide while temporarily insane.

Rainham / Hornchurch

Sixty-year-old Richard Meekins and his wife had been to London to spend Christmas 1875 with their son. On 28 December, the couple returned home to Essex, arriving at Rainham Station at 6.20 p.m. They then set off to walk the rest of the way home but, reaching the small footbridge between Rainham and Hornchurch,

Meekins tripped over a dwarf hedge in the dark and fell headfirst into a dyke.

His head was embedded in the mud at the bottom of the ditch and, try as she might, his wife was unable to pull him free. Eventually, her screams alerted two labourers to her plight and they managed to drag Meekins out of the water, but he had already drowned.

Fulbourn

Thirty-three-year-old William John Amps suffered from epilepsy and mania, as a result of which he was an inmate of the Cambridgeshire County Asylum at Fulbourn.

On 19 December, members of staff were preparing to put up some Christmas decorations and some branches of yew were brought in. A few of the leaves dropped off and, before anyone could stop him, Amps put them in his mouth and swallowed them.

Within an hour, Amps was taken ill and died in spite of the attentions of the Asylum's medical attendant, Mr Rogers, and his assistant. Rogers was unsure about what precisely had killed him, later telling the coroner that the deceased's signs and symptoms were not inconsistent with epilepsy but the presence of leaves in his stomach pointed to the possibility that the narcotic effect of the yew may have hastened his death.

Lowestoft

Fisherman George Saunders and his wife Esther Susannah of Lowestoft, Suffolk, went to town together on Christmas Eve 1885, calling in to see her father on their way home at about nine o'clock that evening. Less than an hour later, their neighbour heard screaming coming from their cottage and, when she went outside to see what was happening, she met Esther running towards her mother's home.

'He's done for me now,' Esther commented as she raced past Mrs Mills, blood gushing from a wound in her throat. Esther bled to death within thirty minutes, during which time her husband walked to the nearest police station and gave himself up.

Charged with his wife's murder, Saunders made a long, rambling statement claiming that Esther saw other men, communicating with them by prearranged signals to let them know when he went out. 'Put me out of my misery. I wish to be hung,' he insisted.

According to the police, Saunders was suffering from *delirium tremens* at the time of the murder and the inquest on his wife's death learned that he was a very heavy drinker, who was polite and gentle when sober but transformed into a mad man when he drank. His father suffered bouts of insanity and eventually committed suicide, and witnesses described Saunders himself as '. . . a rather singular man', adding that he grew worse during the full moon. However, it was not for the inquest to determine Saunders's mental state and a verdict of wilful murder was returned against him.

By the time he appeared before Mr Justice Hawkins at the Suffolk Assizes, his dependence on alcohol had been broken by his incarceration and he seemed very remorseful about the murder. There was no doubt about his guilt, so the main question for the jury to consider was whether or not he was sane at the time of the offence. A doctor and Fellow of the Royal College of Physicians had twice examined Saunders in prison and believed that he was delusional and insane, but Hawkins seemed sceptical and eventually the jury found Saunders guilty, making no concession to his mental state.

He was sentenced to death and hanged by James Berry at Ipswich Prison on 16 February 1886. His death left three children under six years old orphans.

Westcliff-on-Sea

Evans Chad of Westcliff-on-Sea, Essex formed an attachment with a nurse at the Royal Mineral Water Hospital at Bath, where he had been treated for sciatica. He continued an affair with the woman for some time, much to the distress of his wife, May, who wrote to the nurse and received a letter in return saying that if a wife failed to make her husband happy, it was up to him to find happiness elsewhere.

Chad finally left his wife on Christmas Eve 1926 and on the same day she sent him a telegram: 'Happy Christmas, my darling. Won't you come to me today and start afresh? Can I ring you up?'

Chad's response was terse: 'Decision unalterable. Wishes reciprocated. Suggest conversation unnecessarily painful.' Shortly after receiving her husband's telegram, thirty-four-year-old Mrs Chad committed suicide by gassing herself.

Her body was found at her home with several letters and a twenty-eight-page document, which the coroner likened to a diary. One of the letters was addressed to her husband and read, 'Why have you done this cruel thing and left me alone? I cannot bear it. I have tried so hard. Life is empty without your love.'

Called to give evidence at the inquest, Chad denied that the other woman in his life had anything to do with the breakdown of his marriage, saying that separation had been discussed before he first went to Bath because he and his wife's temperaments clashed. The coroner recorded a verdict of 'suicide during temporary insanity', censoring Chad for his 'most reprehensible conduct' towards his wife.

Littlebury, near Saffron Walden

Twenty-one-year-old Charles Wix was a soldier, holding a commission in the 1st Battalion, 11th Regiment. Normally stationed at Dublin, he came home to spend Christmas 1861 with his family at the vicarage in Littlebury, Essex, before being posted to Canada.

On Christmas Eve, Charles went hunting rats with his brothers Robert and Joseph and a friend, Thomas Moule. They took several dogs with them and, at one stage, the dogs began fighting amongst themselves. Joseph shied a clod of earth at them but it had little effect so Charles and Thomas set about trying to part the dogs. Charles went to hit one of them with the butt of his gun but the dog dodged the blow and the gun hit the ground instead, causing it to discharge, shooting Charles in his right-hand side. Although his brother ran for medical assistance, Charles died within minutes.

An inquest jury later returned a verdict of 'accidental death'.

FIVE

WEST MIDLANDS

Birmingham

Horse slaughterer William Edwards of Birmingham spent all Christmas Eve and most of Christmas Day 1883 drinking and, during the afternoon, he knocked his wife down in a fit of temper, cutting her head open. He then punched her in the face, giving her two black eyes.

When Edwards appeared before magistrates in the New Year, his wife complained that in the past her husband had attempted to cut her throat and had also bitten off the top of one of her fingers, which she later had to have amputated. She had just spent eleven weeks in hospital as a result of his violence towards her and had been discharged for Christmas.

Magistrates awarded her a separation order, stating that her husband must pay 5s a week maintenance. Meanwhile, he was sentenced to three months' imprisonment for the latest violent assault on his wife.

Leominster

By December 1864, seventeen-year-old Emma Smith had been a servant in the household of the Wilkes family near Leominster for six months and was known as a hard-working, industrious girl of good character.

On Boxing Day, Mrs Wilkes happened to go upstairs and saw the young servant struggling to carry a large slop pail. Mrs Wilkes offered to carry it downstairs for her maid, who was quite a slightly-built girl, but Emma raised such strong objections to relinquishing the pail that Mrs Wilkes grew suspicious. The two women engaged in what was almost a tug of war for possession of the bucket, which Mrs Wilkes won and, as she carried it away, Emma burst into tears.

Mrs Wilkes took the bucket straight to her husband, who poked around in the contents with a stick. To his horror, he found that the bucket contained the dead body of a baby and, when he investigated further, Wilkes found not one but three babies.

It was evident that, completely unattended, Emma had given birth to triplets and, as each baby was born she plunged it head-first into the pail of liquid waste. She was immediately arrested on suspicion of murder.

Fortunately for Emma, a post-mortem examination showed that the babies were born dead and she was released from custody without charge. Remarkably, Emma had carried and given birth to full-term triplets without anybody having the slightest suspicion that she was pregnant.

Sedgley

On 27 December 1862, Isaac Thompson of Sedgley, Staffordshire, thrust a sharp-pointed poker into the head of his eight-year-old daughter, causing a fatal wound about half an inch wide and between two and three inches deep. What made Thompson's actions more deplorable was that, at the time, he was awaiting trial for roasting another of his children alive and, only fourteen months earlier, was charged with unlawfully wounding a third child.

Thompson first appeared before magistrates in August 1862, after he smacked his thirteen-year-old daughter Rachel in the mouth and threw a metal spike at her, which penetrated one inch into her back. Thompson excused his actions by claiming that his wife was a drunkard who neglected the family and that he was angry at his daughter for leaving her siblings crying when she was supposed to be caring for them. Magistrates sympathised with Thompson for having 'a thorough bad wife' and fined him just 5s with costs.

Only two months later, Thompson took seventeen-month-old Martha downstairs to feed her. The next morning, he asked Rachel where the baby was, having forgotten where he had put her. Martha was eventually found lying dead and badly burned on the floor near the fire. Her father made a statement, relating that his 'thorough bad wife' was out drinking and had neglected to feed the children. He got Martha up and shared his food with her then, suddenly needing to use the lavatory, laid her down on the rug. When he returned, he sat down and, before he knew it, he was asleep.

The inquest jury returned a verdict of manslaughter against Thompson, who was allowed bail until his trial at the Stafford Assizes. It was while on bail that he 'accidentally' threw the poker at eight-year-old Hannah, having come home from the pub and found his 'thorough bad wife' not at home.

Thompson was tried in March 1863 for having feloniously killed and slayed Hannah, which was, of course, a terrible accident 'of a most lamentable kind' that was all the fault of his 'thorough bad wife'. Thompson himself '. . . had been kindly and indulgent to his children and had tried so far as he could to supply the mother's place and it was not to be supposed that he could ever have contemplated injuring his child'.

The jury found Thompson guilty but recommended mercy on account of his 'thorough bad wife'. The prosecution then informed the jury that there was another indictment against Thompson for having killed Martha in October 1862, adding that they did not propose to offer any evidence against him on that charge.

Accordingly, the judge ordered the jury to find Thompson 'not guilty' of the manslaughter of his daughter Martha. For taking Hannah's life Thompson was sentenced to two weeks' imprisonment with hard labour, the sentence to be backdated one week.

Brettell Lane Station, near Stourbridge

Richard and Mary Ann Danby were bidding farewell to their daughter at Brettell Lane Station, near Stourbridge in the Black Country on Christmas Eve 1876. As the train began to pull out of the station, Mary Ann rushed forward to give her daughter one last kiss. Unfortunately, she slipped, falling between the train and the platform.

Although the train was stopped as quickly as possible, forty-three-year-old Mrs Danby was crushed and terribly mutilated, dying within a few minutes. Her husband and daughter witnessed the accident and her untimely death.

Warwick

Forty-five-year-old Mary Hawkes was variously described by those who knew her as 'temperate, respectable, amiable, prudent and sensible.' She worked as a housekeeper for medical officer Dr George Wilson and when Wilson left his house in Warwick in mid-December to visit Brighton, he had no qualms about leaving her in sole charge.

As Christmas neared, Wilson's neighbours became concerned that there was no apparent activity at the house apart from the dog, which seemed to bark continuously. They reported their concerns and, on the evening of Christmas Day, the police forced an entry into the house.

They were met by Wilson's collie dog running excitedly up and down the stairs, carrying a slipper in its mouth. The dog was obviously starving and, when the police went into Mary's bedroom, they found her dead, lying face down on the floor. She was undressed and had obviously been in bed but was now sprawled on a pile of empty port wine bottles.

The corks had been removed from some bottles, while others had been more hurriedly opened by breaking their necks. There were thirty-three bottles in total, including two small ones that stood on a chair with an empty cup. The two small bottles had previously contained poison and it was established that Mary's death was due to poisoning. However, at the inquest on her death, it proved impossible to determine whether she took the poison by accident or by design.

There was nothing to suggest that Mary Hawkes intended to commit suicide and her employer and friends seemed absolutely certain her death was a tragic accident. With no concrete evidence to determine why she died, the jury returned a verdict of 'death by misadventure.'

Birmingham

Luke and Maud Weir lived in a house in Price Street, Birmingham, with their nine children, the whole family sharing one room downstairs and a bedroom upstairs. Luke was an unemployed ex-serviceman, who only had the use of one arm due to old war wounds.

On Christmas Eve 1932, one of the children was staying with friends and another was at a hostel. That left Mr and Mrs Weir and seven children sleeping in the bedroom, when fire broke out in the early hours of the morning. Woken by the flames, Luke roused his wife then tried to get downstairs to fetch help. Finding the staircase ablaze, he jumped out of the first floor window, clad only in his shirt, and ran through the streets until he found a policeman.

When the fire brigade arrived at the house, it was burning fiercely. Maud Weir had jumped from the bedroom window with her baby in her arms but it proved impossible to rescue any of the other children, who, it was later discovered, were suffocated by the smoke. Their charred remains were removed from the house once the fire was extinguished. Maud and the baby were both badly burned, but were believed to have survived. Luke Weir was also burned while trying to rescue his children, as were two firemen.

Luke junior (13), John (12), Rose (8), Theresa (5), Bridget (4) and Terence (2) perished in the blaze and, at the inquest, it was demonstrated that the downstairs room in which the entire family lived measured 11 feet x 11 feet and was 8 feet high. The bedroom, where all eleven normally slept was 11 feet x 11 feet and was 7 feet 4 inches high. Although the family were poor, Mr and Mrs Weir had tried to put up some Christmas decorations in the downstairs room and, although no definitive cause was ever established for the tragedy, it was supposed that the decorations might have caught fire.

Note: Some accounts of the fire name the three youngest children as Terry (7), Theresa (5) and Francis (4). There is also some variation between newspaper reports in the children's ages.

Wednesbury

Seventeen-year-old domestic servant Hannah Mason from Wednesbury was a sturdy girl with a fresh, ruddy complexion. However, in 1894, sturdy, fresh and ruddy weren't fashionable and every girl aspired to being pale and thin.

Somebody told Hannah that, in order to look good, she should drink vinegar and eat starch, raw oatmeal and uncooked rice. Hannah embraced the diet wholeheartedly and it soon had the desired effect – she became pale and thin but, not surprisingly, she also became unhealthy and suffered from constant pain in her side.

When she died on Christmas Eve, the cause of death was given as a perforation of the stomach resulting from an abscess. The inquest jury returned a verdict of 'accidental death' and the coroner strongly condemned the foolhardiness of young girls in pursuit of beauty.

Burslem

On Christmas night 1912, a fire broke out at a house in Burslem, Staffordshire. Seeing smoke issuing from the property, two men managed to gain access through a bedroom window. They found four children in the bedroom – two-year-old Horace Webb was in bed, while his siblings George (10), Lily (5) and Ada (7) had crawled under the bed.

The fire had broken out in the kitchen and, although the flames had not reached the children's bedrooms, the room was filled with smoke. The children were carried outside where it was discovered that only Ada was still alive, her three siblings having been suffocated by the fumes. Sadly, Ada later died in hospital.

The fire was believed to have been caused by paper chains being hung too close to a gas lamp in the kitchen.

Birmingham

Henry Kimberley and Harriet Stewart had cohabited for seventeen years until Christmas 1884, when they decided to separate. Determined to be civilised and amicable, they consulted solicitors and agreed that Harriet would keep the house, while Henry got the piano and the couple's savings of £20. Contracts were signed and almost immediately Kimberley had second thoughts and begged Harriet to reconsider but she was determined to end the relationship.

On 27 December, Henry saw Harriet and her friend, Emma Palmer, going into The White Hart Inn, which was run by Mrs Palmer's husband. Kimberley followed and again asked Harriet to come back to him, but she again refused. He turned to Mrs Palmer and asked her, 'Won't you persuade her that I love her still?' and when she declined to interfere, Henry pulled out a gun and shot both Harriet and Mrs Palmer. A barman tried to disarm him and was fired at but the pub's customers rushed to help and the gunman was subdued until the police arrived

Harriet Stewart survived but Emma Palmer was mortally wounded and died in hospital twelve days after being shot. Henry Kimberley was tried for murder at the Birmingham Assizes and, having been found guilty, was hanged at Winson Green Prison by James Berry on 17 March 1885.

Winson Green Prison, Birmingham, 1934. (Author's collection)

Spernall

The Crowley family of Spernall, Warwickshire, lived in fear of twenty-eight-year-old James, who was the youngest son of William Crowley by his second wife. In the past, James had made countless threats to kill his older brother and father, who eventually made him an allowance of £1 a week and gave him a horse on condition that he moved out of the family home into a cottage on the farm. James agreed, but it didn't stop him from tormenting his father, who moved one of his labourers, William Tilsley, into his home as protection against his wayward son. Crowley even had Tilsley sworn in as a constable, to better deal with James.

Shortly before Christmas, James appeared at his father's house demanding money. As usual, he was violent and abusive and, although he eventually returned to his cottage, William sent Tilsley after him to warn him not to come back. Not unexpectedly, James ignored the order.

On Christmas Day 1841, James approached the farm on foot, carrying his shotgun. As Tilsley and another two workmen tried to protect William and his family, James raised the gun and fired, shooting Tilsley through the head and killing him instantly, before mounting his horse and galloping off.

An inquest returned a verdict of wilful murder against James, who by that time had fled the area and gone to America. In March 1844, he moved back to England and took up residence with a woman but after an argument, his lover betrayed him to the police, who arrested him in The Castle and Falcon public house in Chester. He was armed with a pistol at the time and freely admitted that he was guilty of shooting Tilsley, saying that he would do the same again tomorrow.

Tried at Warwickshire Assizes in April 1845, the only hope for his defence was to show that he was insane at the time of the murder. Although several people testified that James Crowley had a certain 'wildness' and sometimes exhibited 'strange ways', there was nothing to convince the jury that he was insane and he was found guilty. He was hanged at Warwick Prison on 18 April 1845.

Birmingham 🌿🍂🌿

Cecilia Duffy had been suffering from chronic bronchitis for about a fortnight and on 21 December 1857 she asked a neighbour, Helen McNeil, to collect some things from the chemist for her. Helen was given a list and, as instructed, bought two pennyworth of white wine vinegar, two pennyworth of oil of peppermint, two pennyworth of oil of almonds, one pennyworth of oil of aniseed, two pennyworth of syrup of rhubarb, two pennyworth of tincture of rhubarb and one pennyworth of syrup of squills. Then Helen went to another shop, where she purchased a halfpennyworth of common sulphur and half a pound of treacle.

The ingredients were shaken together in a bottle, after which Helen gave a teaspoonful to her own child, who also had a cough.

On Christmas Eve morning, Cecilia and her twenty-year-old daughter, Catherine, were found dead. Dr David Johnson was called and found the two women lying in the same bed. Their faces looked peaceful, as if they were sleeping, but their jaws were rigidly locked and their hands clenched tightly into fists. Johnson, who had seen Cecilia only two days before her death, thought then that her bronchitis was much improved. He suspected that she and Catherine either died from asphyxia or from poison and a post-mortem examination revealed that both mother and daughter had died from ingesting prussic acid.

The home-made cough mixture was in a bottle by the bed, with the cork removed. Johnson distilled some and found that, as he suspected, it yielded prussic acid, which he believed resulted from an adverse reaction between the oil of almonds and the white wine vinegar. He denied that he had suggested that Cecilia Duffy should take any medicine at all and had certainly recommended none of the ingredients in her home remedy. Furthermore, since Catherine was not ill, there was no earthly reason for her to have taken the medicine at all.

At the inquest, Helen Neil stated that, on seeing the two bodies, she felt a little faint and had taken a large swig of the cough medicine as a restorative. Helen insisted that she felt no ill effects at all but the inquest jury believed the scientific evidence, which suggested that the ingredients of the medicine combined to produce something highly toxic, and returned a verdict that both women were accidentally poisoned.

Fenton

Christmas 1871 was proving an absolute nightmare for the Neal (or Neale) family of Fenton, Staffordshire, since they had recently lost a six-month-old child and were waiting for a funeral to be organised.

Labourer Thomas Neal went out on Christmas Eve, returning home at about four o'clock in the morning of Christmas Day roaring drunk. With difficulty, his wife got him into bed and when he woke up two or three hours later, she reprimanded him for his unseemly conduct, reminding him that it was Christmas and they had a dead baby in the house awaiting burial. Thomas was not in the least bit contrite – he shouted at his wife and hit her, so frightening the couple's three-year-old son that the little boy began to cry. Neal rounded on his son and swore at him, threatening to murder him if he didn't shut up. This made William cry even harder and his infuriated father backhanded him with his fist, catching the little boy on his chest and rupturing his diaphragm.

William died almost instantly, leading to his father's arrest. Thomas was charged with manslaughter and sat through the inquest and his appearances before magistrates looking sullen and showing very little emotion. Tried at the Stafford Assizes in March 1872, Thomas admitted killing his son but insisted that it was done unintentionally. Sadly, the only witness to little William's death was his mother and, since she was married to Thomas, she was not permitted to give evidence against him. The prosecution had no way of proving the case and the judge had no alternative but to direct the jury to acquit the defendant.

Hereford

In the early hours of Christmas Day 1843, a fire broke out in the stables of The Green Dragon Hotel in Broad Street, Hereford. More than thirty tons of hay and straw were stored there and the fire took hold very quickly.

The Green Dragon Hotel, Hereford. (Author's collection)

Saving the building was a hopeless task, so firefighters focused on trying to prevent the fire from spreading to adjacent premises and on rescuing the seventeen valuable horses belonging to the London–Bristol Mail Company stabled there.

Four were literally roasted alive and another three were so badly burned that they were unlikely to survive. The remaining ten were rescued, although all had lost their manes and tails and had most of their coats singed completely away.

Chasetown

At six o'clock on the morning of 23 December 1882, three men were admitted to the cage at number 3 Pit of the Cannock Chase Colliery Company, Staffordshire, to be lowered into the mine to feed the horses before the day's work started in earnest. The cage had only descended about 5 yards when the wire rope supporting it snapped and it fell 150 yards to the bottom of the shaft. When it hit the bottom, it broke through the timber flooring covering a sump well, which contained several feet of drainage water.

It took until three o'clock that afternoon to drain sufficient water from the sump to retrieve the bodies. Fifty-year-old Thomas (or George) Collis was married with six children, nineteen-year-old Francis Horton was a single man and twenty-six-year-old Herbert Grimley had been married for less than a week.

The 3-inch diameter rope was only two months old, of the highest quality and had recently been tested according to regulations with two tons of coal. There seemed to be no reason why it should have broken and an inquest jury eventually returned a verdict that '. . . the deceased lost their lives through the breaking of the pit rope.'

Birmingham

At around four o'clock in the morning of Christmas Day 1863, a man looking out of his window on Little Hill Street, Birmingham, noticed that the shutters of The Hill Street Tavern were on fire. Joseph Payne hammered on the pub door until he roused landlord George Gameson, who went downstairs to investigate. There was no smoke or flames and Gameson could see nothing apart from a light shining under the front room door, but, when he opened the door and allowed air into the room, the fire suddenly exploded and roared out of control.

Almost instantly the stairs were alight, trapping the other occupants of the house upstairs. Unable to reach them, Gameson managed to open the front door and collapsed onto the street. As soon as he recovered, he shouted for help and before long several members of the Borough Police Force arrived at the pub.

Servant Elizabeth Hancox (or Hancocks) told fourteen-year-old Matilda 'Tilly' Gameson, 'Jump for your life, Tilly,' but while Elizabeth jumped, Tilly was afraid to follow her. Mrs Gameson was helped down from her bedroom window on a ladder procured by a neighbour and her thirteen-year-old son John threw his baby brother George out of the window and then jumped himself. Sadly, several members of the family failed to escape the inferno. Tilly died in the blaze, along with her sisters, seven-year-old Betsy and nine-year-old Emily and her two-year-old brother, William. The children's nursemaid, Amy Spratt, perished, as did a family friend who was visiting at the time, fifty-eight-year-old Sarah Bradbury.

At the inquest on the six deaths, there was some suggestion that the police who attended the fire were drunk and it was also noted that the water pressure was so low that it rendered the fire-fighters' hoses ineffective. However, the jury decided that, rather than being drunk, the policemen had been overwhelmed by the hopelessness of the situation. There was nothing to show how the fire started, although George Gameson strongly suspected a defect in the gas supply. However, it was impossible to prove and the inquest jury eventually returned verdicts of accidental death on all six victims.

Worcester

On the evening of Christmas Day 1895, several people in High Street, Worcester, saw forty-six-year-old clergyman Charles James Hinkson apparently place his hand under the skirt worn by eleven-year-old Florence Davis. Hinkson, who was said to be 'very much the worse for liquor', was followed and apprehended by concerned members of the public, who handed him over to a passing policeman.

Charged with indecent assault at Worcester City Sessions, Hinkson admitted that he was a little drunk. He explained his conduct saying that he heard a noise and stopped to ask Florence what it was. While talking to her, he accidentally dropped his walking stick and, as he picked it up, it caught in something.

Witnesses believed that Hinkson deliberately used his walking stick to lift the hem of Florence's skirt before intimately touching the child but he explained that he thought his stick was caught in his cassock and as soon as he realised that it wasn't he walked away. Surprisingly, given the number of witnesses to his actions, the jury gave Hinkson the benefit of the doubt and he was found not guilty and discharged.

Birmingham

On Christmas Day 1875, James Brislin and Edward Walters were involved in a fight in Thomas Street, Birmingham. Brislin was knocked down three times before somebody fetched his father to try and stop the fight. Fifty-four-year-old William Brislin went to pick his son up and, as he was doing so, Samuel Todd suddenly ran up and punched him, knocking him over. While William struggled to his feet, Todd ran into his house and came out wielding a table knife, with which he stabbed William twice in the face, once by his left eye and once by his chin.

William Brislin was taken to hospital, where he died on 31 December and a post-mortem examination revealed that his skull was fractured beneath the wound on his forehead. His death was due to a *contre coup* injury – the blow on one side of his head had caused a ruptured blood vessel on the opposite side of his brain.

Eighteen-year-old Samuel Todd was arrested and charged with wilful murder. He was both deaf and dumb and so struggled to follow the proceedings at his eventual appearance at the Warwick Assizes in April 1876.

Through interpreters, Todd denied having had a knife, although he admitted to throwing a single stone. Surgeons had found three wounds on Brislin's face, one of which they believed resulted from a punch, which drove his upper lip into his teeth. The wound on Brislin's chin was clean cut and had most probably been made by a blade. However, surgeons believed that the wound on his forehead – the fatal wound – had been caused by a blunt object, although they conceded that it could have resulted from a blow from a knife handle.

In summing up the case for the jury, Judge Mr Baron Huddleston instructed them that if they believed that the fatal wound had been inflicted by a knife handle and not a knife, there was sufficient cause for reducing the charge from murder to manslaughter, on the grounds that death was not the natural and probable conse-quence of such a blow and therefore a knife used in that fashion was not necessarily a deadly weapon. The jury considered this for around five minutes before finding Todd guilty of manslaughter. He was sentenced to fifteen years' penal servitude and was sent to Portland Prison in Dorset to serve his sentence.

Worcester

Henry Blundell came to Worcester to visit his mother and sister, who kept The Crown and Anchor Inn, and on Christmas Day 1873, he and three friends hired a boat for a pleasure trip up the River Severn.

The men sailed for a couple of miles before calling at a public house, where they all drank plenty of beer before starting the return journey. Sadly, their boat capsized and all four men were thrown into the river.

On seeing them struggling in the water, people on the river banks sprang into action. William Blundell, John Overton and Isaac Cooke were pulled out of the water unconscious but are believed to have survived. Sadly, by the time Henry Blundell was dragged to the bank he had drowned and it proved impossible to resuscitate him.

Blundell was thirty-two-years-old and had been in the navy for fifteen years, rising to the rank of Petty Officer. He was considered a very good swimmer.

Elkstone

Fourteen-year-old Mary Hulme, who was in service in Staffordshire, was allowed some time off over Christmas 1906 to visit her family and on Boxing Day, Mary's mother, Hannah, walked to Leek market to meet her.

After leaving Leek at five o'clock in the afternoon, they reached Thorncliffe an hour later. A mile past Thorncliffe, it began to snow heavily and mother and daughter stopped at a friend's house for some tea to allow the worst of the weather to pass. When they resumed their journey, it was still snowing but before they had walked over two fields, the blizzard suddenly worsened again. The pair took refuge in a henhouse for three hours before the snowstorm abated sufficiently for them to try and continue walking home.

The Hulmes had barely walked across the first field after the henhouse when the blizzard started afresh and they were unable to tell where they were or determine in which direction they should be walking. Confused and disoriented, they blundered about until they got stuck fast in a snowdrift and were unable to move.

They huddled together all night in the fierce snowstorm, which was accompanied by thunder and lightning and heavy winds and, as dawn broke, Mary recognised that they were only a couple of hundred yards from home and that there was a farmhouse close by. She tried to rouse her mother but Hannah didn't stir and soon Mary realised that her mother was dead.

A post-mortem examination showed that her death was due to exposure and an inquest jury returned a verdict in accordance with the medical evidence.

Birmingham

On Christmas Day 1858, jeweller William Thornton went to The Hope and Anchor Brewery, Birmingham, where he sat enjoying a glass of beer and smoking his pipe. The landlord, Mr Southall, was an old friend and, seeing Thornton, he sent out a plate of roast turkey from his own dinner table for him.

Minutes later, Southall saw Thornton race past the window of the bar and, when Southall went to see what had prompted Thornton to run away, he found him lying on his back on the road outside the tavern.

Thornton appeared to be dying and although a surgeon was summoned, he was unable to save him. A post-mortem examination showed that Thornton had a piece of turkey more than four inches long and weighing more than an ounce lodged in his throat, which had suffocated him. At the subsequent inquest the jury returned a verdict of 'accidental death from gorging'.

Warwick

When Sidney and Mabel Gardner asked their mother what she would like as a Christmas present, she did not hesitate. Having previously kept a parrot as a pet, she told her children that she would love to have another one and so, on 19 December 1929, Mrs Gardner went into Birmingham and chose a green parrot, for which she paid £4 10s.

On New Year's Day 1930, the family woke up to find the bird dead in its cage. The following day, Mrs Gardner took it back to the shop and was given a replacement but that too died a day later.

On 7 January, Mrs Gardner complained of feeling very tired and took to her bed. Five days later, she was still unwell when her husband appeared to go down with a cold, and, by 15 January, fifty-eight-year-old Charles Gardner was delirious. When he heard about the parrots, the couple's doctor suggested that both the Gardners were admitted to Birmingham General Hospital as a precaution and, on 19 January, Sidney Gardner fell ill and was also hospitalised.

Although Mrs Gardner and Sidney ultimately recovered, Charles Gardner died on 20 January from pneumonia and septicaemia. Tests on the parrot's cage isolated numerous dangerous bacteria, but the inquest jury were not entirely convinced that he contracted his fatal illness from the parrot and returned a verdict of 'death from natural causes'.

Birmingham General Hospital. (Author's collection)

Wolverhampton

On Christmas Eve, forty-six-year-old Daniel Onions was working as a furnace man at Blackwell's Works in Wolverhampton. The furnaces were equipped with tuyers – openings which allowed blasts of air into the furnace to facilitate combustion – and when some water accidentally got into the tuyer, the furnace exploded, sending a shower of molten metal all over Onions, who was dreadfully burned and subsequently died from his injuries.

An inquest later returned a verdict of 'accidental death', although the dead man's work mates preferred to view it as Divine retribution for an act of gross barbarity. Some weeks before his death, Onions was seen to throw the foal of an ass into the furnace, where it was roasted alive.

EAST MIDLANDS

Stanfree

Christmas was a very special time for Richard Stanley Morris, since Christmas Eve was also his birthday and, in 1947, he spent it at his family home in Stanfree, Derbyshire, with his fiancée Sybil Marriott.

There were about half a dozen people in the living room, watching as Richard and Sybil filled Christmas stockings for the family's children. Richard, who had recently been troubled by poultry thieves, was keen to show his family a gun that someone had lent him but, unbeknown to Richard, not only was the gun loaded but it also had a very light trigger pull and rather than shooting poultry thieves, Richard's next act was to accidentally shoot his fiancée dead.

At the subsequent inquest, the witnesses who testified were in no doubt that the shooting was entirely unintentional and the coroner accepted that Miss Marriott's death was a tragic accident. 'You will remember it all your life and that will be sufficient punishment for you,' he told Morris, as the jury returned a verdict of 'accidental death'.

Leicester

Six-month-old Harriet Elsie Hancox was a delicate baby and on Christmas Day 1894, her mother took her to the doctor thinking that the child was having convulsions. Dr Emmerson thought that Harriet was suffering from little more than indigestion.

Feeding baby, 1900s. (Author's collection)

The baby was writhing in pain and when Emmerson asked what her mother had been feeding her, Mrs Hancox admitted that the infant had been eating Christmas pudding.

The doctor was appalled. He gave Mrs Hancox some medicine for Harriet and some advice on feeding and suggested that she should place her daughter in a warm bath to ease her pain. As instructed, Mrs Hancox fed her daughter nothing but diluted milk but Harriet died within forty-eight hours and Dr Emmerson believed that her death was due to convulsions, arising from improper feeding.

At the inquest on Harriet's death, the coroner was shocked to learn that until Christmas Day, Harriet's diet consisted of little more than boiled bread.

'Are you not aware that plum pudding is a most improper food for a child six months old?' coroner Robert Harvey asked Mrs Hancox.

'She seemed to crave it,' answered Harriet's mother

'But did you not know it was an improper thing?' the coroner persisted.

'No, sir.'

The coroner told his jury that he found it difficult to believe Mrs Hancox's ignorance of childcare, although he had no doubt that the Christmas pudding was kindly meant. When the jury found that Harriet died from improper feeding, Harvey merely advised her mother to be more careful in the future.

Heighington

Widow Mrs Hammond was awakened in the early hours of 28 December 1898 by the smell of smoke. Realising that her house in Heighington, Lincolnshire was on fire, Mrs Hammond roused her five children and told them to follow her outside.

When she got out, she realised that only three of the children were with her and, since the fire didn't seem too serious, she sent ten-year-old Henry 'Harry' Charles back inside to find his brother and sister while she raised the alarm. However, the house was made from wood and once the flames caught hold, it burned like a furnace.

When the fire was finally extinguished, Harry was found near a window, clutching five-year-old Beatrice Maude in his arms. Sadly, nine-year-old George Edward was burned to a cinder. There was nothing to suggest what caused the fire.

Denby

Eleven-year-old William Horsley was employed underground, driving one of the asses at the Denby Old Colliery Pit in Derbyshire. On 23 December 1835, part of the roof of the pit fell and William was crushed beneath the rubble. He was fatally injured and died where he lay within minutes.

The roof had been inspected a very short time before the accident and was considered to be in a perfectly safe condition. Thus when junior coroner Mr Whiston held an inquest on Christmas Eve, the jury returned a verdict of 'accidental death'.

Lutterworth

On Boxing Day 1870, George Holt and Samuel Loomes went out shooting birds at Lutterworth, Leicestershire. Holt took aim at a fieldfare in the hedgerow but missed. Ignoring the fact that one of the barrels of his double-barrelled shotgun was still loaded, Holt began to reload. He was holding the gun upright when the loaded barrel fired, almost literally blowing his head off. Only the back part of his skull was left intact and, according to the contemporary newspaper accounts of the tragedy '... his brains were strewn about the greensward on the roadside.'

Loomes was standing about 3 yards away at the time and was liberally splattered with blood and gore. Realising that he could not help his friend, he ran as fast as he could to alert the local police and Holt's body was taken home in a cart to await the attentions of the coroner. The inquest jury returned a verdict of 'accidental death', blaming twenty-four-year-old Holt's carelessness with his gun for his tragic demise.

Groby

Labourer Thomas Gilliver (or Gilbert) of Groby, Leicestershire, attended a wedding on Christmas Day 1858, at which he became so intoxicated that he was unable to walk. His nephew and another man eventually escorted him home, unlocking the door of his house for him since he was incapable of doing so himself.

Nothing more was heard of Gilliver until 29 December, when, not having seen him about, his neighbours went to check on him. They found him sitting cross-legged in his fireplace, which he had apparently mistaken for a chair.

He had slumped forward and his mouth and nose were tightly pressed against one of his thighs, stopping him from breathing. Doctors found that he had suffocated '. . . while in a state of helpless intoxication' and an inquest jury later returned a verdict in accordance with the medical evidence.

Great Longstone, near Bakewell

Farmer Edward Wager of Great Longstone, Derbyshire, was a brute of a man. His wife divorced him on the grounds of his cruelty and he had served several prison sentences for violent assaults. In 1866, Wager married his second wife, Harriet, and soon began abusing her too.

On Christmas Eve 1866, a female neighbour came to visit and Edward tried to take liberties with her. The woman's cries of protest brought Harriet running and, not surprisingly, she was angry and told Edward that if he did things like that, she would leave him. Edward was not used to being told what he could or could not do and showed his displeasure with his fists.

As the visitor fled, she could hear Harriet screaming and, minutes later, two men working nearby heard shrieking and saw her run out of the farm, her face covered in blood. Edward followed closely behind her, beating her as she ran away. Harriet called to the men for help but they were too afraid to interfere and merely watched as she fell to her knees and begged her husband for mercy.

Instead of tackling Wager, the workmen set off to fetch a policeman. As they looked back, they saw Harriet topple into a stretch of water known locally as the Vein (or Veil) Dam.

It was not clear if she accidentally fell into the water or if she was pushed but Edward made no attempt to rescue her. ''Er's in the dam,' he remarked casually to the two workmen, before returning home and opening a bottle of gin. Although the water was only around 5 feet deep, the workmen felt it was beyond them to try and save Harriet and it was left to the police to drag her dead body from the pool.

Harriet was covered in cuts and bruises, with one particularly bad injury to her upper lip, the centre of which was completely missing. In addition, her nose and upper jaw were broken and her liver was ruptured. Since she had been fleeing Edward's violence when she died, he was charged with her wilful murder, appearing at the Derby Assizes on 6 March 1867.

The jury found him guilty, although they tempered their verdict with a recommendation for mercy on the grounds that Harriet threw herself into the water. When the death sentence was pronounced, Edward left the dock laughing.

The contemporary newspapers were extremely scathing about the cowardice exhibited by the two men who stood by and watched Harriet's murder. They were incredulous when, just before his scheduled execution, the Home Secretary commuted Wager's death sentence to one of life imprisonment. 'If ever a man deserved to swing from the gallows, it is Edward Wager,' wrote the *Telegraph*.

Frodingham

A blacksmith's forge was situated under an archway at the Frodingham Iron and Steel Company in Lincolnshire and, on 27 December 1892, without any warning, the arch suddenly collapsed, burying five men under several tons of rubble.

The men were thought to have died instantly and the blacksmith, John Southwick, was found with his tongs still in his hands,

whereas the other men's bodies were so mutilated that they could only be recognised by their clothes.

Southwick, Moses Parker, Joseph Shucksmith, William Hobson and John Simpson were all married men with families, Shucksmith alone having seven children. Moments before the arch fell, Southwick's son was talking to his father and consequently witnessed the accident that claimed his father's life.

Nottingham

In the early hours of the morning of Christmas Eve 1889, a man walking along Ilkeston Road, Nottingham spotted a fire burning in one of the shops. The premises was a three-storey building, with a tailor's shop on the ground floor and living quarters for the owner and his family on the first and second.

By shouting and banging on the door, the passer-by succeeded in rousing Meyer Gadian and his wife Annie, who were asleep on the top floor. Meyer threw open the bedroom window to see what the man wanted, then made the fatal mistake of opening his bedroom door. The resulting current of air drew the fire up the staircase, instantly blocking the Gadians' only escape route.

The couple tried to throw their mattress out of their bedroom window to cushion their landing but the window was too small and eventually both husband and wife jumped into the street below. Both suffered major injuries, which included fractured skulls, and, although they were rushed to Nottingham General Hospital, Gadian died shortly after his admission and his wife died a few hours later. The couple had been married for just six weeks.

The fire brigade were quick to arrive at the Gadians' premises and the fire was soon extinguished. When the property was inspected, the damage to the living room on the first floor was minimal. The living room door had remained shut throughout and it seemed likely that if the Gadians had only kept their bedroom door closed, they would have survived to be rescued by the fire brigade.

Before jumping from the window, Mrs Gadian threw out a portmanteau containing cash and jewellery. It was immediately snatched up by Sarah Shaw, who ran away with it and was later prosecuted for theft.

Bakewell

Samuel Wyatt, the groom at The Rutland Arms Inn at Bakewell, Derbyshire, went to tend the horses on Christmas Day 1860 and found a dead woman in the stables. There seemed little doubt that the woman had met with foul play, yet a post-mortem examination showed that she was also riddled with disease, suffering from heart failure, dropsy and a chronic liver condition.

The woman was a vagrant named Mary Ann Wilson, who was travelling to join her husband who worked in the Derbyshire lime kilns. An inquest was held on her death by coroner Mr Bennett, at which several navvies who were drinking in the town on Christmas Eve testified, even though they were cautioned by the coroner. One, William Cook, also known as 'Gloucester Bill', said that Mary had asked him if she could go home with him on Christmas Eve. Cook's lodgings did not permit female visitors, so he took her to the stable, where she apparently begged him to lay down with her because she was so cold.

Cook admitted to having sexual intercourse with Mary, saying that he then fell asleep until she woke him some time later to say that there were other men in the stable. The men supposedly threatened Cook and he went back to his lodgings. (There was little doubt that Mary had intercourse with more than one man on the night of her death.)

By the end of the inquest, several men had been charged with Mary Ann Wilson's manslaughter. In addition to manslaughter, Cook, Wyatt the groom, John Sheldon, William Eaton, William Wheeldon and George Whitehead were also charged with assaulting and ravishing the deceased.

When the case came to trial at the Derby Assizes in March 1861, the Grand Jury threw out the indictment for assault and ravishing and the men faced only the manslaughter charge. There was insufficient evidence against Whitehead, and the remaining men were acquitted due to the impossibility of proving that the frail, sick woman did not die a natural death. 'I should not have been surprised at the sudden death of such a woman,' stated the surgeon who carried out the post-mortem.

In discharging the prisoners, the judge remarked wryly that he hoped this would be a warning to them not to drink too much at Christmas in the future.

Leicester

Although John and Daisy Tolley had not yet been married for a year, their union was far from happy and Daisy had twice taken her husband before magistrates for beating her. The most recent occasion was in December 1893, when magistrates dismissed the case, in the belief that there was fault on both sides. However, husband and wife decided to separate and Daisy moved back to her parents' home in Blue Boar Street, Leicester.

Tolley made a couple of visits to his wife's parents' home to talk about what should be done with the couple's possessions and on 23 December he arrived at the house to find his wife and her mother, Mrs Kendall, doing housework. He seemed to want to

discuss some blankets and, after
a few minutes, the conversation
grew heated. All of a sudden,
Tolley jumped forward and seized his wife's throat,
putting a gun to her head and firing.

'He's killing my Daisy!' Mrs Kendall shouted, as
Tolley fired a second shot into the back of his wife's head. Tolley
left his wife lying on the floor and walked into the front room,
closing the door behind him. While the neighbours debated
what to do next, someone outside noticed splashes of blood on
the window blind of the room into which Tolley had fled. The
door was barricaded from the inside with chairs but when it was
forced, Tolley was found dead on the floor, his throat cut.

Although comatose, nineteen-year-old Daisy Tolley was still
breathing and a doctor advised her removal to the Infirmary.
However, by the time she arrived, she was dead, the cause of her
death being gunshot wounds to the head.

Coroner Mr Harvey opened an inquest on the two deaths that
evening, which he adjourned after hearing the medical evidence.
When it resumed five days later, the jury were told that Tolley was
a spinner and a former soldier, having served six years in India
before his honourable discharge two years earlier, after which he
worked as a dyer's labourer until three weeks before the shooting.

At thirty, he was much older than his wife and was acutely
jealous. The separation, coupled with his inability to find a job
seemed to have made him despondent and, on the morning of
the shooting, he borrowed a gun from a friend.

The inquest jury needed only a few minutes to return a verdict
of 'wilful murder by John Tolley' in respect of Daisy Tolley's death
with *felo de se* – an archaic term meaning murder of oneself – in
respect of John Tolley's own demise.

Nottingham

When Mrs Marshall looked out of her bedroom window on
Christmas Eve 1937, she saw smoke coming from the house
occupied by the Whyley family in Henry Street, Nottingham.
Her husband scaled the wall between the back yards of the two

Nottingham from the castle. (Author's collection)

properties and, unable to rouse the family, began knocking down the back door. He was joined by another neighbour but once the door was opened the men were driven back by the heat and intensity of the fire.

Fifty-year-old Frank Whyley jumped 35 feet from a first floor window, landing in the yard. He was taken to hospital unconscious but died a few minutes after admission.

Firemen were quickly on the scene and raised ladders to the windows in the upper storey but were driven back by flames and smoke whenever they tried to enter the house. It took thirty minutes to get the fire under sufficient control to be able to get inside the property, where firemen found Mrs Rose Whyley and the Whyleys' daughters, fifteen-year-old Lily and eight-year-old Florence. All had been suffocated by the smoke.

Northampton

The Northampton borough coroner held an inquest on Christmas Eve 1888 on the death of feather dealer Alfred Preston.

Fifty-six-year-old Preston was walking from one room in his house to another when the tall hat that he was wearing failed to pass underneath the door lintel. The hat was forced down onto

Preston's head and he shouted in pain until his family helped him remove it.

Since he was still in pain after being divested of his hat, a doctor was summoned, but, in spite of medical treatment, Preston died. A post-mortem examination later showed that the cause of his death was injury to his brain due to the compression of his skull by his hat.

The inquest jury returned a verdict of 'accidental death'.

Sutton-in-Ashfield

In the early hours of Christmas Day 1894, Sarah Oldham wandered through the back door of her sister Keziah Dove's house in Sutton-in-Ashfield, Nottinghamshire and slumped in a chair without speaking. When Keziah looked at her sister, she saw that she was dressed in her nightdress, the front of which was saturated with blood.

Keziah's screams brought her husband downstairs. He ran to Sarah's house, a few doors up the street, returning with Sarah's partner, Edmund Kesteven. Someone else had gone for a policeman and, when Sergeant Henry Sills arrived, Kesteven told him calmly, 'I did it. You will find it upstairs what I have done it with. It is broken.' Sills later retrieved a broken razor from the bedroom shared by Sarah and Kesteven.

Surgeon John Stavely Dick was sent for but Sarah had bled to death before he arrived. He later conducted a post-mortem examination, finding a three-and-a-half inch long wound on the right-hand side of Sarah's throat, which had severed her jugular vein. The wound could have been self-inflicted if Sarah were left handed but, since she was not, the jury at the inquest on her death

found a verdict of wilful murder against Kesteven, who was committed for trial at the Nottingham Assizes.

Sarah Oldham was actually married to another man but had separated from her husband some years earlier and he now lived in America. She and Kesteven had been living as man and wife for almost four years and seemed to get on very well together, although he could be jealous and sometimes accused her of seeing other men. Both shared a fondness for drink although both were said to be sober on Christmas Eve. Sarah, Keziah and another sister went shopping together, parting company only a couple of hours before Sarah's death. Sarah visited a neighbour at half-past eleven on Christmas Eve, when she was said to be sober and quiet – less than an hour later she was dead.

At Kesteven's trial, there was some suggestion that Kesteven was insane and numerous witnesses were called to give examples of his past strange behaviour, including a doctor who stated that he was prepared to send Kesteven to an asylum eleven years earlier. Nevertheless, the jury found him guilty of wilful murder and Kesteven told the judge that he would rather die than be sent to an asylum for the rest of his life. He got his wish and was executed at Nottingham on 26 March 1895.

Gainsborough

In 1845, cakes and sweetmeats were often doctored with jalap, a herb used for keeping the bowels open and, at Christmas in Gainsborough, Lincolnshire, three children from the Murray family were taken ill after eating what was known locally as 'laughing gingerbread'.

It was never established whether the children had eaten an excess of gingerbread, given to them by 'a thoughtless girl', or whether they were unlucky enough to have eaten a batch to which an exceptionally large quantity of jalap had been added. Whichever was the case, the children were stricken with acute sickness and diarrhoea and one died on 26 December, the second a day later. The third child, who was older, made a full recovery.

Chapel-en-le-Frith

On Christmas Day 1892, a party of young men drank until half-past-two in the afternoon at The Hat and Feathers in Chapel-en-le-Frith in Derbyshire. They left when the pub closed, taking with them three pint bottles of whisky and rum, which they consumed in a wooden shed in a yard behind The Royal Oak Hotel.

While all of the men were drunk, two actually passed out due to the effects of alcohol and, when their friends decided to go home and were unable to rouse them they just left them where they were, hoping that they would sober up.

At about nine o'clock that night, one of the men realised that he had lost his pipe and went to look for it. He tripped over William Birchenough and George Hibbert, who were still lying on the floor. Birchenough was frozen to death, while Hibbert was semi-conscious, his hands frozen to the ground.

Both men were taken into the hotel, where strenuous efforts were made to revive them. After attempting artificial respiration for thirty minutes it was evident that Birchenough was beyond assistance, while Hibbert's condition was described at the time as 'precarious', although he is believed to have survived.

At the inquest on twenty-two-year-old Birchenough's death, after recording a verdict that the deceased was frozen to death, coroner Mr Davis condemned what he called 'a disgraceful carousal', for which the deceased had paid with his life. He called on the doctor who treated the two young men in the hotel to dispel once and for all the myth that drinking spirits kept out the cold.

Bolsover

The children of Bolsover enjoyed a special treat on Christmas Eve 1910 – a cinematograph performance had been laid on for them at the Central Hall, Carr Vale. The performance ended just after five o'clock in the evening and a crocodile of fifteen children walked back from Carr Vale to Bolsover, singing Christmas carols as they went.

In order to reach Bolsover, the children had to cross the Great Central Railway line at a level crossing. As always, when a train approached, the main level crossing gates were shut and locked but a wicket gate at the side was left open. The children waited as a passenger train passed and pulled up at the station a few yards further down the line. Then, assuming that it was safe to cross, they walked through the wicket gate onto the line. They failed to see an empty goods train, which ploughed into them.

Their screams brought people dashing up the line from the station. Brother and sister, Joseph William and Mary Margaret Bacon, aged ten and nine years old respectively, lay dead on the track and another child had been carried almost 30 yards, his body so mutilated that it was almost impossible to identify until, by process of elimination, it was found to be that of eight-year-old George Alfred Boot. Three more children were seriously injured, although all survived.

An inquest exonerated the train driver, who was completely unaware that the accident had occurred. He was travelling at a moderate speed and had blown the train whistle continuously as he approached the crossing. It seemed as though the passenger train had drowned out the sound of the approaching goods train, giving the impression that it was safe to cross.

The Carr Vale crossing was notoriously dangerous. It was frequently used by schoolchildren and there had been narrow escapes there in the past. The Great Central Railway Company had already been approached by the local Urban District Council to request a footbridge or a subway but it seemed impossible for the two parties to reach agreement and, so far, five different schemes had been put forward and ultimately rejected. The Christmas tragedy served to emphasize the urgency of making such an arrangement and it was agreed that a foot subway would be constructed and a permanent guard placed on the crossing until work was completed.

Anstey

On Christmas Eve 1928, Emma Black left her three children alone at home in Anstey, Leicestershire, while she popped out to do some last minute Christmas shopping. When she returned twenty minutes later, she found the house in darkness and the

couch smouldering, the living room full of thick smoke. Three-year-old Margaret and two-year-old Avice were sitting on the couch dead, while the baby was crawled on the floor.

An inquest on the deaths of the two girls surmised that the gas-powered lights had run out and the children were not able to put a penny in the slot meter to restore the gas supply. In darkness, they lit a piece of paper at the fire and accidentally set the Christmas decorations alight.

The two girls were suffocated by the smoke, the baby escaping because it was at floor level and, since the smoke rose, it was still able to breathe fresh air.

SEVEN

YORKSHIRE AND HUMBER

Hull

At about half-past seven on Christmas night 1860, the Master of the sloop *Hope*, which was moored in Queen's Dock, Hull, saw sparks issuing from the ship's hold. Mr Bayes (or Rayes) threw some water down into the hold and then went to investigate.

The ship carried a cargo of potatoes and a fire had been lit in the stove to prevent them from freezing. In front of the stove, Bayes found the body of James Dent, a destitute orphan boy of about fourteen, who occasionally sneaked on board vessels in the docks to get warm and sleep. James had literally roasted in front of the fire – the waist of his trousers was burned and the skin on his face, right arm and side had swollen to bursting point.

Bayes had checked the stove only about an hour earlier and Dent wasn't there then. An inquest determined that he had tried to warm himself and been accidentally suffocated by the fumes in the confined space of the hold.

Sheffield

Coroner Mr Webster held an inquest in Sheffield on Christmas Eve 1866 on the death of four-year-old Benjamin Russell Scott.

Two days earlier, Ben was somewhat feverish and his mother sent her maid, Annie Morris, to the druggist's shop to purchase a powder. When Annie got to the shop, there was another maid waiting to be served, who had been sent to collect a powder for an adult.

Mrs Huddlestone, the druggist's wife, prepared the morphia powder for the adult. The intended recipient was a morphine addict, who specifically asked that the packet containing her powder was not labelled. Meanwhile, Mr Huddlestone made up the fever powder for Ben.

Just as he finished wrapping it, someone rushed into the shop and called Huddlestone to a nearby house, where a child was in grave danger of choking to death on a boiled sweet. The druggist managed to save the child before hastening back to his shop where, in his agitation, he accidentally swapped the packets of powder, selling the morphia to Annie Morris. Huddlestone's mistake was only discovered when the woman who should have received the morphia sent her maid back to the shop. Although Huddlestone went straight to the Scotts' home, Ben had already been given the powder and died soon afterwards.

The inquest found that Benjamin died from the accidental administration of a quantity of morphia. Although they believed that Huddlestone had shown a lack of attention and caution, they did not believe that he had been criminally negligent, although they recom-  mended that no druggist should ever allow poisonous drugs to be sold without being clearly labelled. The irony of the situation did not escape the contemporary newspapers, which were quick to point out that in saving the life of a little boy who was choking Huddlestone had inadvertently caused the death of another child.

Carlin How, Cleveland

Between ten and eleven o'clock at night on Christmas Eve 1873, a woman walking from Brotton to Carlin How in Cleveland noticed a number of young men hustling an elderly woman through a gate into a field. When she asked what they were doing, she was told that the woman was very drunk and that they were putting her behind the hedge to sober up, out of the way of passing traffic.

On Christmas morning, a man passing the field saw a woman's shawl hanging on the gate. Curious, he looked into the field and saw bloodstains. He alerted the police, who searched the field and found numerous personal articles, including a doll, an orange, a bonnet, a handkerchief and a screw of tobacco. The ground inside the field was scuffed and spattered with blood, as if a great struggle had taken place, the scuff marks leading to an open shaft belonging to the Loftus Ironstone Company.

At the bottom lay the battered body of a woman, almost every bone in her body broken. She was later identified as a female tramp, Mary Ward, who had been walking round the village on Christmas Eve singing carols for money. She had been raped before her death.

In the course of their enquiries, police questioned seventeen-year-old Henry Shaw. Asked if he knew anything about the woman found dead in the shaft, Shaw made a voluntary statement in which he admitted to having intercourse with Mary Ward, while two of his friends held her legs open.

Since the police had not released information that Mary was raped, Shaw was arrested on suspicion of causing her death, as were his friends James 'Jud' Fleming, George Bowler, Joseph Carter and Thomas Knight. However, since Mary was known to have been very drunk on Christmas Eve, it was impossible to prove that she hadn't accidentally wandered into the pit, rather than been thrown in. Thus the men were charged only with rape, and at a special sitting at Guisborough, magistrates determined that Bowler and Knight should be discharged, while Shaw, Carter and Fleming should stand trial at the York Assizes.

They appeared before Mr Justice Archibald in March 1874, Shaw charged with rape and Carter and Fleming charged with aiding and abetting him. The only real evidence against Carter and Fleming was Shaw's statement and the jury found them not guilty. Shaw was found guilty and sentenced to ten years'

York Assize Courts. (Author's collection)

penal servitude, which he served at Rochester Borstal Prison in Kent.

Batley

On Christmas Eve 1886, the Batley Tradesmen's Association of West Yorkshire organised an event in the market place, which concluded with a spectacular display of fireworks. People pushed forward for a better view and a barrier holding back the crowd was knocked over. Unfortunately, in the melee, someone accidentally kicked over a mortar firework, which exploded in the crowd.

Six boys were injured, among them thirteen-year-old Frank Sykes, who was badly burned on his hands and lower body and had both of his legs shattered. He died in agony at eleven o'clock that night. A second boy had his right leg blown to smithereens and it was later necessary to amputate it, although he is believed to have survived.

Rotherham

Nine-year-old Phoebe Stevenson of Rotherham could hardly contain her excitement. Her older brother, William, had bought some raffle tickets in her name and, on 23 December 1874, the draw was about to take place.

Phoebe asked her mother if she might go and watch the prizes being awarded and her mother was happy to let her go. Just minutes later, the child was carried back into the house by neighbours, who saw her fall over in the street and not get up.

A doctor was summoned but by the time he arrived, Phoebe was dead. It was later established that she had tripped over a bucket and broken her neck.

Redcar

During a severe gale on Christmas Day 1836, the Danish brig *Caroline* was seen to be in difficulties off Coatham Sands and the Redcar lifeboat, *Zetland,* was launched to go to her aid.

The crew left *Caroline* in two small boats, which were quickly overwhelmed by the high seas. Had they stayed with the ship, they would probably have survived, since it was eventually washed up on sands at the mouth of the River Tees. As it was, all ten crew lost their lives, as did pilot William Guy from the lifeboat, who was swept overboard as he tried to throw a line to one of the crew.

Guy, whose body was not recovered for almost six weeks, left a wife and four children to mourn his loss. He has the distinction of being *Zetland's* only fatality during her long history of rescues.

Leeds

Forty-five-year-old herbalist James Carling's business had been failing for some time. To better his prospects, he sold his home and moved to Philadelphia, where he got a good job. Unfortunately, he was only there for three weeks when he fell ill and had to return to England.

Every penny he had was spent on his passages to and from America and when he arrived back in Leeds he was so despondent that his wife was afraid to leave him alone with their children, fearing that he might do something rash. However, on 23 December 1882, Carling persuaded her to take a trip into town to look at the Christmas decorations, suggesting that if she stayed out until midnight she may be able to purchase some cheap meat for the family's Christmas dinner.

Mrs Carling returned home at half-past eleven and found the door locked. She knocked but there was no response and, assuming her husband and children had gone to bed and were sleeping soundly, she stayed the night at her sister's house. When she returned home on the morning of Christmas Eve and was still unable to rouse anyone, she fetched a joiner and got him to break into the house.

Inside, James Carling was lying in bed with his two daughters. Eight-year-old Julia Carling was dead, her three-year-old sister Hannah Elizabeth was barely breathing and James himself was semi-conscious. Naturally, Mrs Carling went to summon a doctor and, as soon as she left the room, her husband took his razor from a drawer and cut his own throat.

By the time the doctor arrived, he had bled to death and although every effort was made to save Hannah, she too died later that day. A post-mortem examination showed that she died from morphia poisoning, while her sister was apparently drugged then strangled.

Carling left three letters, one to his wife, one to his mother-in-law and one to the coroner. The letter to his wife urged her to try and keep up her spirits and do the best she could, whereas the one to the coroner stated that, having suffered from severe pains in his head for several weeks, Carling was almost frantic and wanted only to put an end to his painful existence.

The inquest found that Carling killed his daughters and committed suicide while of an unsound state of mind.

Huddersfield

On Christmas Day 1840, a massive fire destroyed Messrs Roberts Brothers' mill at Spout Fields, near Huddersfield. The fire began in one of the upper storeys and was visible for several miles. It quickly spread through the rest of the building and by the time it was brought under control almost £14,000 worth of damage had been done. However, the building was only insured for £8,000 and the loss of the mill left around 300 local men without jobs.

It was said that the damage would have been much less had the firemen been in a fit state to perform their duties. 'Of the few who came with the engine, most, if not all of them were in a state of nearly complete intoxication,' reported *The Leeds Intelligence*, adding that the firemen were so stupefied that they could not work their own equipment, which was eventually hijacked by members of the public, who were appalled at the incompetent performance of the professional firefighters.

Mill engineer Joseph Barstow lived in a house adjoining the mill and, as the fire raged, he and his family managed to remove most of his furniture and personal belongings from their home, which remained largely untouched by the blaze. On 30 December, Joseph decided it was safe to move back in with his family but, during the night, it grew windy and the walls of the ruined mill were blown onto Barstow's house, demolishing it completely. Barstow, his wife Mary and their two-year-old daughter Zillah were killed.

Middlesbrough

In the New Year of 1876, John Stokes of Middlesbrough, North Yorkshire, appeared before magistrates charged with inflicting grievous bodily harm on his wife, Ann. On Stokes's first appearance in court, Ann was still hospitalised, suffering from the effects of a two-and-a-half inch long wound on her temple, beneath which her skull was visibly dented. So grave was Ann's condition that it was initially feared that she would die and a deposition was taken, in which she stated that on Christmas Day 1875, her husband hit her over the head with a frying pan. Although Stokes vehemently denied the accusation, a witness came forward to say that he had seen Stokes strike Ann twice before she fell to the ground.

Stokes was remanded in custody for one week in the hope that his wife would be fit to appear in court. When she did, her deposition was read to her and she flatly denied ever having told the police that her husband struck her, neither did she say that her husband had knocked her down. All she would admit was that he threw a frying pan and it 'accidentally' hit her but not hard enough to knock her over.

By now, there were two eyewitnesses prepared to swear that they had seen Stokes hitting his wife and magistrates decided that a most brutal assault had been committed. Stokes was sentenced to six months' imprisonment with hard labour and ordered to pay the court costs, with an extra two months in prison if he didn't pay.

York

Private Samuel Dunlop and his wife were taking an evening stroll in York on Boxing night 1888 when they heard a woman shouting for help. Dunlop handed his wife his umbrella and book and ran down to the side of the River Ouse. A woman was struggling in the water near the Blue Bridge and although he was unable to swim, Dunlop could not stand by and watch her drown.

Courageously, he went into the river to try and save her but he too was soon in difficulties. People on the bank procured a boat and attempted a rescue but Dunlop and the young woman quickly sank beneath the surface of the water. Their bodies were recovered using drag lines some time later.

The young woman was later identified as Amy Kettlewell, a native of Bradford. Twenty-one-year-old Amy was a domestic servant at Castlegate, York, and had only been in her current position for a week. She was described by her employers as 'pleasant, quiet and well behaved' and came to them with glowing references from her previous employer. Boxing Day was her night off and she left the house shortly after six o'clock, in her normal state of health.

There was nothing to suggest how or why Amy Kettlewell came to be in the river. A public subscription was later started for

Blue Bridge, York, 1905. (Author's collection)

the widow of Private Dunlop, who had been married for only three weeks when she witnessed her husband's death from the banks of the river.

Note: The deaths occurred at the confluence between the Rivers Ouse and Foss. Thus some newspapers report that the couple were drowned in the Ouse, others the Foss.

Bradford

Thirty-year-old George Howarth of Bradford was found dead in a garage on Christmas Day 1925, leaning over the engine of a motor car with his head fast between a revolving shaft and the exhaust pipe. His face was seriously burned by the exhaust pipe and the back of his head had been completely torn away by the revolving shaft. Two friends who had been working with Howarth on the motor car and had gone home for dinner, leaving him alone in the garage, suffered slightly from the effects of the fumes.

Hull

An inquest was held on 23 December 1910 on the death of six-year-old John Wild. His mother found the child with his clothes on fire and although she quickly smothered the flames with a blanket, her son later died from the effects of severe burns. Before his death, he told his mother that his clothes caught fire after he stood on the fender and called up the chimney to Father Christmas. 'I asked him to send me a pair of roller skates, a magic lantern and some candles,' he said. Sadly, the first two items on John's list were already wrapped and hidden at home, waiting to be opened on Christmas Day.

Walkley, near Sheffield

On Christmas Day morning 1877, a match was played between Walkley and St Phillip's football clubs at the ground rented by St Phillip's. The ball was accidentally kicked over the low wall at the boundary of the pitch and one of the Walkley players helpfully vaulted the wall to go and retrieve it. Sadly, twenty-three-year-old George Beaumont wasn't aware that the wall surrounded a quarry and he fell 80 feet to his death.

At the subsequent inquest held by coroner Mr Wightman, the jury returned a verdict of 'death through misadventure', saying that they believed that it was the duty of St Phillip's Football Club to warn strangers to the ground not to leap over the boundary walls in pursuit of the ball.

Hull

In 1884, blind newspaper vendor John Friskin and his wife Jane from Hull had a visitor staying with them over Christmas and spent Christmas Eve enjoying a drink. At just after five o'clock in the morning of Christmas Day, the Friskins and their guest, Hannah Leek, finally retired to bed. By then, Friskin wasn't just blind, he was also blind drunk, and as his wife led him upstairs to bed, he stumbled and fell from the top of the staircase, dragging Jane with him.

They landed in a tangled heap at the bottom of the stairs and, unable to rouse them, Hannah sent for a doctor who pronounced sixty-seven-year-old John and sixty-eight-year-old Jane dead. An inquest heard that the couple had engaged in what the local newspaper referred to as '. . . an injudicious indulgence of seasonable potations' and that both had broken their necks in their fall, dying instantly. The inquest jury returned two verdicts of 'accidental death'.

Bradford

On Christmas Day 1888, a football match took place between Manningham and Heckmondwike at the Valley Parade ground in Bradford. At one point during the game as the crowd surged forward, a wooden railing broke under their combined weight and several young spectators were crushed.

Thirteen-year-old John Varley broke a leg and two other boys suffered sprains and severe bruising but although medical assistance arrived very quickly, it came too late for thirteen-year-old Thomas Coyle, whose neck was broken in the crush.

An inquest was opened but adjourned when the coroner learned that the railings had previously given way in almost the same place. The coroner wanted the structure examined by experts to see if there was criminal negligence by the football club but Coyle's death was eventually deemed a tragic accident.

Leeds

In 1900, thirty-eight-year-old Henry Horner and his wife and children from Dewsbury went to stay with a friend in Leeds over the festive season. A party was held in the house on Christmas Day and, at about midnight, Mr Horner left the gathering to go and look for a lavatory. Walking around upstairs in the semi-darkness, he mistakenly took a wrong turn and plunged headlong down a flight of stairs, breaking his neck. An inquest later returned a verdict of 'accidental death'.

Hornsea

On Christmas Day 1855, cousins Mary and John Warcup and Sarah Bird were expected at a family Christmas dinner. Hornsea Mere was frozen over and they decided to take a shortcut by walking across the ice.

They got about three-quarters of the way across the lake when the ice broke and the two girls fell through into the water. John Warcup ran as fast as he could to get help, while the women clung to the edge of the ice, screaming. The commotion attracted a number of people who amassed ropes and ladders and made every effort to reach them. Mr Leak got close enough to grab the hand of one of the girls but as he did, the ice broke beneath him and he and John Warcup were plunged into the water.

Leak and Warcup were pulled out exhausted and cold but alive. Seventeen-year-old Mary and eighteen-year-old Sarah remained in the water for ninety minutes, until a boat was dragged over the ice and their bodies pulled into it. An inquest held later that evening returned a verdict of 'accidental drowning' on both girls.

Sheffield

Twenty-four-year-old Joseph White from Bletchley in Buckinghamshire was employed as a navvy in the construction of dams for the Sheffield Water Works Company. He and his fellow labourers lived on site in a series of specially erected huts and there was also an on-site 'tommy shop', which sold basic provisions. The shop kept a stock of ale, which they sold by the bucketful.

On Christmas Eve 1852, a party of twelve labourers congregated in one of the huts and, between them, drank five and a half gallons of ale. White drank more than most and eventually challenged one of the other men to a fight. Both combatants were so drunk that the fight was a short one, which ended without apparent injury to either man.

The next morning, White started drinking at seven o'clock in the morning and by ten o'clock was so drunk that he wanted to fight everybody. At various times throughout Christmas Day, White fought fellow workmen Joseph Wood, John Smith, John Brown and a Mr Richings.

After the fight with Richings, somebody took White back to his own hut and sat him in a chair. However, he was incapable of remaining upright and fell forwards, hitting his head on the stone floor. He was put to bed at about four o'clock in the afternoon and spent the remainder of the afternoon and evening snoring loudly.

Each bed in the huts was shared by two navvies and at ten o'clock that night, White's bed-mate, Mr Foster, climbed into bed with him. At two o'clock the next morning, Foster was disturbed by the entrance of another drunken navvy into the hut, at which point Foster realised that White was dead, lying cold and absolutely rigid in bed beside him.

An inquest was opened and adjourned after the coroner ordered a post-mortem examination. Surgeon Mr Moore found that White's death was caused by an extraversion of blood on the brain but found no external marks of violence apart from a few slight bruises. It was impossible to determine whether the bleeding on White's brain occurred naturally or if it resulted from a blow or a fall during one of his many fights, the fall from the chair onto the stone floor, or was caused by excessive drinking. Unable to attribute the precise cause of White's death, the inquest jury returned a verdict that he died from extraversion of blood on the brain but that there was no satisfactory evidence as to what caused it.

Leeds

In 1860, just as Christmas dinner was being served in the home of William Longley of Leeds, the boiler exploded, instantly killing Mrs Elizabeth Longley and severely injuring her husband, daughter and maid. Fortunately, three of the Longleys' children were not at home at the time of the explosion, otherwise there may have been more fatalities.

An investigation suggested that the feed pipe to the cast-iron boiler had frozen, so that the boiler didn't gradually refill as it emptied. The boiler became red hot and when the ice in the feed pipe eventually thawed, the inrush of water generated a quantity of steam that caused the boiler to explode.

Coroner Mr Blackburn opened an inquest on Mrs Longley's death, adjourning it almost immediately so that an engineer might examine what remained of the boiler, which was done on 27 December. John Hetherington found that the boiler was not really fit for purpose, saying that wrought iron boilers should always be used in place of cast-iron ones for hot water apparatuses and that the Longleys' boiler had been made purely for kitchen purposes and, having no safety valve, was never intended to supply water to the upper rooms. The inquest jury returned a verdict of 'accidental death'.

Bradford

On Christmas Day 1893, five-year-old Joseph O'Neil and his older brother were allowed out to play and were joined by another boy. As they were crossing a road in Bradford, a three-horse omnibus suddenly came tearing round a corner and, although Joseph tried to get out of the way, he was knocked over and trampled by the horses. One of his ribs was broken and punctured a lung, leading to his death soon after the accident.

Forster Square, Bradford. (Author's collection)

The omnibus driver, twenty-five-year-old Edmund Jones, made no attempt to stop but instead went straight back to the depot stables. Police interviewed him there shortly after the accident and concluded that he was under the influence of drink and, when the inquest on Joseph's death returned a verdict of manslaughter against Jones, on the grounds that he was guilty of gross negligence, he was immediately arrested.

At his trial at the Assizes, Jones denied being intoxicated, saying that he had drunk half a glass of beer on an empty stomach. His version of the accident was that he walked rather than galloped along the street and that Joseph ran away from his older brother and was trying to board the moving bus when he slipped and fell. This was contradictory to his earlier statement, in which he said that he only saw the two older boys.

There were numerous witnesses to the accident yet each seemed to have different accounts of what took place. The eyewitness accounts were sufficiently at odds with each other to give rise to reasonable doubt in the minds of the jury, who eventually acquitted Jones.

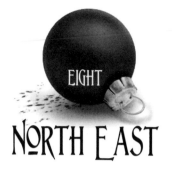

EIGHT

NORTH EAST

Gateshead

On Boxing Day 1898, a group of men were larking about on Highgate Quay, Gateshead, when one of them strayed too close to the edge and fell into the River Tyne. Another of the group promptly stripped off his coat and jumped in to try and save him.

When it became evident that both men were in difficulties, a third man went into the river and managed to grab the first man and bring him to the shore. Sadly, the man was dead and his rescuer exhausted.

By chance deputy coroner Mr Shepherd was present when the body was brought to the mortuary and held an immediate inquest. Although at that stage, the victim had not even been identified, the inquest jury returned a verdict of 'found drowned'.

The body of the second man to enter the water had not yet been retrieved but his coat and cap on the quay were recognised by his sister, who told the inquest that her brother, Robert Armstrong, was twenty years old and had been out of work for three years, during which time he had been desperately seeking employment. He was due to start a job the next day.

Sunderland

Forty-one-year-old John William Moss and thirty-three-year-old Mary Ellen Calder cohabited in Sunderland. Both had been married before and had children, Mary having five.

In December 1875, Moss's son George Pickering Moss came to live with his father, at which time he was a stout, healthy five-year-old. However landlady Mrs Crozier soon noticed a change in the boy. She frequently remonstrated with Moss and Mary about their ill-treatment of George and was threatened for not minding her own business.

Mrs Crozier seems to have been aware that George was being beaten and starved for many months and although she offered to take him and look after him free of charge, she does not appear to have alerted the authorities to the child's plight.

Eventually, on 20 September 1876, somebody finally tipped off the police about little George and a constable arrived to see him. George was dirty and poorly clothed and the policeman described him as looking more like a monkey than a child. A doctor was called in and found George to be neglected and malnourished. He suggested to Mary that she should try and get the child into hospital but Mary insisted that she couldn't afford to do so. A second surgeon saw George twice in November 1876 and told Mary that the child was starving but she claimed that he had all he needed to eat.

When George died on Christmas Eve 1876, he weighed just eighteen pounds, whereas a child his age would normally weigh between thirty-six and forty-five pounds. The cause of his death was given as starvation and the inquest jury returned a verdict of wilful murder against Moss and Mary Calder.

They were tried at the Durham Assizes in February 1877, before Lord Chief Justice Coleridge. Surprisingly, the Grand Jury threw out the bill for murder hence the couple were tried for the lesser offence of manslaughter.

Coleridge was enraged at the conduct of the officials involved, asking the jury who was really guilty of starving George. Was it his parents, who had no money to buy food, or was it the police officers and doctors who effectively stood by for three months and let the child die?

The jury found Moss and Mary Ellen Calder guilty of man-slaughter and Coleridge sentenced them each to fifteen years' imprisonment. He concurred with the jury, who recommended some form of censure for the doctors and police officers, saying that he personally could do little more than disallow their court expenses but added that he would be writing to the appropriate authorities in due course.

Durham

Twenty-eight-year-old Stephen Bartle was well- known in Durham since, in spite of being completely blind, he worked as a milkman for the Cleveland Dairy Company selling milk on the streets and, with his sister-in-law, was also the landlord of The Masons' Arms public house.

On Christmas Eve 1880, civil engineer James Craggs visited some friends in Durham and went for a drink in Bartle's pub. As Craggs was sitting down, he accidentally bumped against a table and two glasses fell to the floor and were smashed.

Bartle demanded payment for the glasses but as thirty-seven-year-old Craggs put his hand in his pocket to take out his money, Bartle seized him by the scruff of the neck and the seat of the trousers, frogmarched him to the door and threw him out. Craggs fell onto the flagstone footpath, at which Bartle slammed the pub door, leaving him sprawled on the ground.

When he didn't get up, a young man went to the police station 50 yards away and fetched PC Stoker (or Stokoe), who found Craggs unconscious and bleeding and called out the police surgeon. Craggs was sent to hospital, where he died from a fractured skull on Christmas Day.

An inquest returned a verdict of manslaughter against Bartle, who was tried at the Durham Assizes in January 1881. It being Christmas, the pub was crowded and, although there were a great many witnesses, most seemed to have seen completely different incidents. There was disagreement as to whether Craggs was drunk or not and if he was about to pay for the glasses, had refused to pay, or was simply arguing about whether or not he was responsible for the damage. Some witnesses believed that

Craggs was about to hit Bartle with his walking stick and some stated that Bartle had asked Craggs to leave but he refused to go. Some said that Craggs was ejected straight out of the pub door, while others thought that he grabbed the door frame and put up a fierce resistance.

It was fairly obvious that Bartle had never intended to kill Craggs and the jury found him guilty of manslaughter but added a recommendation for mercy. He was sentenced to six months' imprisonment with hard labour, which he served in Durham Prison.

Low Pittington

On 23 December 1869, Hannah Harrup and her sister from Middle Rainton, County Durham, went to visit friends at Coxhoe. In the mid afternoon, the two elderly women set out to walk back to Middle Rainton, a journey of around twelve miles.

There were deep snowdrifts and the sisters found the going arduous, so much so that when they stopped to take tea at Sherburn at about six o'clock, Hannah was 'attacked by a fit'. Nevertheless, the two women left Sherburn at between seven and eight o'clock to walk the last four miles of their journey home.

The snow was between 2 and 4 feet deep and eventually sixty-six-year-old Hannah seemed to suddenly lose the use of her limbs and sank onto the snow exhausted. Her sister tried to pull her to her feet but without success and so returned to Sherburn for assistance.

Unbeknown to the sisters, Hannah had collapsed just outside Low Pittington, so the villagers at Sherburn directed her back to the village constable there. She reached the police house at half-past one in the morning of Christmas Eve and told PC Miller where to find her sister.

The constable traced Hannah and lifted her into his arms but the snow was too deep for him to carry her, as he sank deep into the drifts with every step. He moved her into a sheltered position, covered her with his greatcoat and went back to the village, from where he summoned the parish constable, Mr Punshon. Hannah was still alive and together the two policemen carried her to the village pub on a stretcher. A surgeon was called to attend to her but sadly by the time he had made his way through the snow, Hannah had died.

In reporting the tragedy, the *Newcastle Journal* mentions that another elderly lady was missing from the area and it was presumed that she had lost her way in the snow and died from exposure, as did Hannah Harrup.

Gateshead

James Ingles and his wife Elizabeth spent most of Christmas Day 1881 drinking at the home of their friends John and Catherine Lane. Late at night, they left the Lanes' house with a friend, Mary Ann Barnes, and returned to their own home in Gateshead, County Durham. Mary Ann left for a while and, when she returned, she found that James had beaten Elizabeth senseless. She was put to bed, where she quickly lapsed into unconsciousness and died two days later, when a post-mortem examination showed that she had a fractured skull, having been hit on the head with a three-legged stool.

James Ingles fled the area but was soon captured and tried at the Durham Assizes in January 1882. Charged with manslaughter, the jury found him guilty but recommended him to mercy on the grounds that Elizabeth had provoked him and Ingles was sentenced to five years' penal servitude. He and his wife had been married only four months at the time of her death.

Newcastle-upon-Tyne

On Boxing Day 1873, around fifty men were travelling to work on board the steam tug *Gipsy Queen*. As the boat passed Northumberland Dock on the River Tyne, it struck a submerged hopper that was accidentally sunk the night before.

The tug sustained so much damage that it sank within five minutes. Many men were sheltering from the cold below decks and as soon as the alarm was raised, the gangways and passages became blocked by men trying to escape. The *Gipsy Queen's* lifeboat was launched but such was the rush to board it that it capsized.

The quayside, Newcastle-upon-Tyne, 1917. (Author's collection)

Some men were picked up by a nearby dredger, some swam ashore and six men clung to the tug's funnel and were later rescued. One man was towed ashore by the captain's retriever dog but eighteen died in the tragedy, most married men with children.

An inquest heard that the hazardous sunken hopper was well lit and that the *Gipsy Queen's* crew had been warned of its existence. The inquest found that the men were drowned by the sinking of the *Gipsy Queen*, the steamer at the time being improperly navigated, but there was no evidence to show why she was off her course.

Littletown

John Thompson spent Christmas Day 1938 on duty at RAF Usworth and so missed his seven-month-old son's first Christmas. When John returned home that night, he was met by the tragic news that his wife Bertha was dead, her body laid out on the kitchen table of the house in Sherburn Hill that she and her husband had occupied for just three weeks.

John was told that his wife and her parents had gone for a walk that afternoon with Bertha's two brothers and younger sister. As they neared the reservoir at Littletown, County Durham, they were drawn to the water by the sounds of children screaming and realised a little boy had fallen through the ice.

Bertha immediately thrust her baby at her mother and set off to try and rescue ten-year-old Joseph Turnbull, who was the son of her neighbours. She got within a couple of feet of the boy before the ice broke and she joined him in the water.

Bertha's father, Mr Cook, and her two brothers Albert and Edward waded in. Mr Cook managed to grab Joseph and pull him to the bank, before returning for Bertha, who was hauled out of the water and onto Alfred's back. Sadly, as Alfred was carrying his sister to safety, he stumbled and she fell back into the water and disappeared.

Meanwhile, twenty-two-year-old Joseph Kennedy had run for a rope, which he tied around his waist. He dived down into the icy water, finding Bertha tangled in weed at the bottom and, on his third attempt he managed to free her. Just as the couple reached the surface, the rope broke and both Kennedy and Bertha Thompson sank. Two more bystanders went to try and rescue them but they too fell into the reservoir.

By now, someone had fetched a ladder and the two latest casualties were pulled from the water, followed by Joseph Kennedy, who was still clutching Bertha. Kennedy managed to hang onto a rung of the ladder with one hand and Bertha with the other and was dragged to safety. Apart from the cold, Kennedy suffered no ill effects from his immersion in the water but Bertha Thompson was dead.

Gateshead

The pantomime 'Aladdin and his Wonderful Lamp' was being performed to a packed house at the Theatre Royal in Gateshead when, out of the blue, a woman shouted 'Fire!' In an instant, the theatre was in the grip of a spreading panic – women screamed and fainted and there was an uncontrolled dash for the exits.

From the stage, the performers appealed for calm but the crowd were beyond listening to reason. As the exit corridors became blocked, people were crushed, trampled underfoot or suffocated as the patrons fought desperately to escape.

Some men broke windows to allow fresh air into the building, while others attempted to hold back the crowds. Ticket collector Thomas Forster tried to calm people down but was crushed to death and another group of men rushed to tackle the fire, which was nothing more than a dropped match that had fallen through the floor and set light to some sawdust – it was extinguished in seconds with a bucket of water.

When the uproar died down, there were nine children dead, along with twenty-nine-year-old Forster, who left a widow and four children. On 4 January 1892, the incident claimed an eleventh victim, when Frank Goodwin died from injuries received when jumping out of a window to escape what he imagined was a devastating fire. One of the most tragic accounts of the disaster came from a policeman who was one of the first of the emergency services to reach the scene. The policeman picked up an injured child to carry him out of harm's way only then realising that the boy was his own son, Archie Waddington, who died minutes later in his distraught father's arms.

To add insult to injury, the cast of the pantomime were forced to escape the theatre in costume and, when they later returned to their dressing rooms, their normal attire had been stolen.

An inquest later laid the blame for the tragedy on the unknown woman, whose scream caused such blind panic. They returned a verdict '... that the fire which caused the panic was caused by the culpable act of some person or persons unknown.'

Tynemouth

On Christmas Day 1858, Mr and Mrs Robson and their children went to visit the children's maternal grandmother, Mrs Gibson, at her home in Tynemouth. In the evening, it was intended that there would be a party for all the children, with a magic lantern show.

The two youngest children were nine-month-old twins and, during the afternoon, one baby fell asleep while being nursed by a maid. To save her holding the baby, a folding bed was placed in the parlour and the child put down to sleep in it. However, it refused to settle and began to cry and the maid took it out of the bed.

Meanwhile, Mr Robson had been nursing the other twin and, when that baby fell asleep, he placed it in the folding bed.

Mrs Gibson saw the maid take the baby out of the bed but didn't see her son-in-law put the other twin in and so folded the bed up and put it away without realising that there was still a baby asleep in it. Soon afterwards, Mr Robson noticed the bed was missing and asked where the baby was – the bed was retrieved but the baby had suffocated.

Mrs Gibson, who was described as '. . . a kind and affectionate old lady', was beside herself but an inquest held by coroner Mr Reed absolved her of all blame, the jury returning a verdict of 'accidental death'.

Durham

Twenty-one-year-old Herbert Appleby was hanged at Durham Prison on Christmas Eve 1952.

Herbert was courting Lilian 'Dolly' Robbins and on 20 September 1952, the couple went to a friend's wedding together. Herbert was acting as the best man and, at the reception, he saw Dolly sitting on a sofa next to the groom's stepbrother, John David Thomas.

Jealously overrode reason and, convinced that Thomas was trying to muscle in on Dolly, Herbert picked up a kitchen knife and stabbed him, before getting into a taxi and asking to be taken to the police station.

At Herbert's trial for murder at the Assizes in Leeds, the defence tried to prove that he was insane at the time of the killing. He was known to sleepwalk and was very moody, threatening suicide on more than one occasion and even making an unsuccessful attempt to end his own life in 1950. Epilepsy ran in his family and he also had a squint, caused by instruments used to deliver him at birth, which it was suggested may also have caused some brain damage. However, the medical officer at Durham Prison told the court that in his opinion, the murder was down to nothing more than bad temper fuelled by drink and the jury agreed, finding Herbert Appleby guilty.

Cockerton, near Darlington

On 27 December 1878, neighbours became concerned when nobody appeared to be up and about at the Devlin family's rented rooms in Cockerton, County Durham. They alerted the police and, after getting no reply to his knocks, Sergeant Collingwood forced the door. Upstairs, he found fifty-year-old Edward, his wife Mary and two of their children, seven-year-old John Thomas Devlin and his eight-year-old sister Christiana dead, leaving thirteen-year-old Catherine the only survivor.

Devlin had fallen on hard times, mainly due to his own intemperance and he and his wife had been advised to go into the workhouse, which they both said they would rather die than do. The weather was extremely cold and, in order to keep warm at nights, fifty-year-old Edward Devlin would light a bucket full of coke, which he stood on a piece of iron in the centre of the bedroom shared by his whole family. At the same time, he sealed the door and windows and stuffed the chimney with old sacks to prevent draughts.

The cause of all four deaths was given as suffocation, caused by a build-up of the fumes from the coke fire in the badly ventilated room. Catherine survived only because she was furthest away from the stove and, at the time of the inquest, was still seriously ill in hospital.

Coroner Mr J.T. Proud heard all sorts of rumours and gossip at the inquest, including suggestions that the family had been drugged, that Edward Devlin was insane and had beaten and abused his wife and children and eventually murdered them. Eventually the inquest jury determined that '. . . the Devlins met their death from suffocation, caused by the fumes of gas coke.'

Sunderland

On Christmas Day 1889, Mary Adams of Sunderland went to collect water from a standpipe and was surprised to see a woman lying flat on her back in the yard, apparently sleeping off an excess of alcohol. When Mary got closer, she recognised the woman as her own mother and, removing a fur tippet from the woman's face, made the shocking discovery that she had been brutally murdered.

Fifty-year-old Isabella Taylor's forehead had been split open with an axe
and a mass of brain matter and clotted blood extruded from the wound.

The yard entrance was through
a narrow passage between the houses
and police were told that Isabella had vomited in the passage. When they checked, they found Isabella's house key in
the vomit, while her shawl lay nearby. She had been carrying a shopping basket containing packets of tea and sugar and,
although the tea was untouched, the sugar was missing and was
later found concealed in the roof of a lavatory in the yard.

Isabella visited her daughter on Christmas Eve, leaving around
half-past ten at night, saying that she was going home. Instead she
went to a nearby pub, where the landlady refused to serve her
as she was drunk. From there she went back to the yard, where
doctors believed that she was murdered between four and five
o'clock on Christmas morning.

At the inquest on her death, some startling evidence was given
by eight-year-old Frances Gillens, who lived with her family in
the same building as Mary Adams. Frances saw Mrs Taylor dancing and singing in the yard at about one o'clock in the morning
and, two hours later, she saw her father lifting her up. According
to Frances, William Gillens told Mrs Taylor to go away but she
wouldn't so he came back indoors and asked her grandmother for
her axe, which was kept in a cupboard.

The coroner adjourned the inquest and Frances was allowed
home with her parents. When the inquest reconvened on
6 January 1890, there were rumours that Frances had been beaten
and she refused to say anything further. Her grandmother, Eleanor
Pearce, and mother testified that the little girl was lying, while her
father said very little.

An axe was removed from Mrs Pearce's rooms and although it
fitted the wound on Isabella's head perfectly, there was not a trace
of blood on it.

Eventually, the inquest recorded a verdict of wilful murder against
some person or persons unknown and the murder remains unsolved.

Newcastle-upon-Tyne

On Christmas night 1888, nine-year-old Edward Quinn's mother put him to bed, kissed him goodnight and gave him something to drink. Within a short while, both Edward and his mother Matilda had agonising stomach pains and, when questioned, Matilda admitted to having poisoned her son.

The police were sent for and Superintendent Moss from Ouseburn police station arrived at the house and quickly took charge. He sent Matilda's husband out to buy fresh milk, which he gave to Edward in the hope of diluting the poison. Moss then summoned the police ambulance and Edward and his mother were taken to hospital, where Matilda told doctors that she had steeped matches in water, producing a solution of phosphorous, which she fed to Edward and then took herself.

Matilda had written a suicide note, which read:

> I am going to poison myself. I can't live any longer. I could not think of leaving little Neddie behind me and when I am dead do not look at me or yet follow my funeral, for I hate you for what you have done to me and my children. Give my boots and what other clothes I have to Mrs Robson. I am sorry I did not go to see

Newcastle-upon-Tyne, 1914. (Author's collection)

my mother on Saturday, for she is the only friend I have in this life. Whoever reads this letter tell Ned he can have his fling. He ruined me and my children. I was only three months married when he injured me. God will curse him for what he has done to me and mine. The lying brute.

Good night – MATILDA WILKINSON.

Put little James's hair in the coffin beside me.

Luckily for Matilda, neither she nor her son succumbed to the poison and, after having their stomach's pumped, both made a full recovery. Matilda was tried at the Assizes at Newcastle-upon-Tyne in February 1889, charged with administering poison with intent to murder and, found guilty, was sentenced to four months' imprisonment.

Blyth

An inquest was held at Blyth, Northumberland on Christmas Eve 1932 on the death of three-year-old Maggie Archbold, the daughter of an unemployed shipyard worker. Intending to decorate their house for Christmas, the family gathered some boughs of holly, which were placed in the back yard of their house.

After playing out there for a while, Maggie suddenly fell ill with severe gastro-enteritis and, although a doctor was called, she died before he arrived. The cause of the child's death was the ingestion of a toxic substance, most probably holly, a fatal dose of which was said to be around twelve berries.

NINE

NORTH WEST

Westhoughton

The Hulton Colliery Company employed almost 2,500 men, 900 of whom descended into Pretoria Pit at Westhoughton, Lancashire, on 21 December 1910. At just before eight o'clock in the morning, there was a tremendous underground explosion that was believed to result from a miner's lamp igniting accumulated firedamp gas and coal dust from an earlier roof fall.

There were five coal seams named Trencherbone, Plodder, Yard, Three-Quarter and Arley and of the 345 miners working the Yard seam, only four were brought to the surface alive. Of these, Fountain Byers survived less than twenty four hours.

The youngest victim of the disaster was thirteen years old and

almost two-thirds of the dead were under twenty. A 200-yard stretch of road in the village of Westhoughton was home to seventy-three of the victims and many families in the area lost more than one member – one family from Wingates lost the father and five sons, while John Thomas Houghton from Chequerbent died with three of his sons, the youngest of whom, Frederick Stanley Houghton, died on his first day at work in the mine.

One body was identified by two family members as being that of William Lord. However, unbeknown to his family, Lord was working at a mine in Barnsley and, on reading of his own death in the newspaper, sent a terse telegram to his wife reading, 'Alive Woman. Send to pit at once.'

A memorial to the deceased was constructed in Westhoughton Cemetery, where 171 of the victims were buried, and there were various other memorials, including a plaque at Westhoughton Town Hall, erected by the Bolton and District Cricket Association, which commemorates the loss of fifteen players or committee members. In 2010, a memorial was erected at Westhoughton by the town council to mark the centenary of the tragedy.

Wigan

On Christmas Eve 1894, six-year-old Andrew Matthewson of Holland Street, Wigan in Lancashire, excitedly hung his stocking on the mantelpiece at bedtime in anticipation of a visit from Santa Claus.

When Andrew woke in the morning, he was delighted to see that he had not been forgotten. Sadly, as he stood on the fender to take down his stocking, his clothing caught fire and he sustained such severe burns that he died in hospital that afternoon. An inquest later returned a verdict of 'accidental death'.

Saddleworth

On 23 December 1865, twenty-eight-year-old Matthias Robson travelled to Saddleworth by train to visit friends for the Christmas holidays. The train was an especially long one, since it was not only a Saturday night but there was also an extra demand for travel during the festive season. Hence, when the train stopped at Saddleworth, only the front part of it was actually at the station.

Having heard the porters calling out the name of the station, Robson got off the train as soon as it stopped. He had been chat-

Saddleworth viaduct, 1912. (Author's collection)

ting companionably to the other passengers in his carriage and, having stepped off the train, he turned round to bid them good-night. As he did so, his feet slipped from under him.

Only then was it evident that, instead of disembarking onto the station platform, Robson was actually standing on top of a low stone wall running along the top of a viaduct. He plummeted backwards to his death, landing on a road almost 70 feet below the viaduct and fracturing his skull and several limbs.

At the inquest on Robson's death it was revealed that another passenger had also got off the train onto the wall but, being a native of Saddleworth, realised his mistake when he stepped up instead of down as he normally would when disembarking onto the platform. Fortunately, he managed to get down from the wall safely.

The inquest jury returned a verdict of 'accidental death' but recommended that the parapet wall should be securely fenced and the station platform lengthened. They also strongly recommended that there should be an additional porter on duty at the station at night.

Chadderton

Three-year-old Arthur Keith Parry of Chadderton, Lancashire, was suffering from whooping cough on Christmas Eve 1930 and, since his mother was out working, he was left in his father's care for the day.

When it was time for his son's medicine, Arthur Parry took the bottle down from the shelf, carefully measured the required dose and gave it to the child. The boy asked for some sugar to take the taste away and, as his father was fetching some, he heard his son choking. Only then did Parry realise that he had accidentally given Arthur creosote instead of his medicine. The boy was bundled into a taxi and rushed to Oldham Royal Infirmary but died later that day.

At the inquest on his death, both parents were absolutely distraught. Mrs Parry had purchased a bottle of creosote with the intention of fumigating the room but had not mentioned her purchase to her husband. The creosote and medicine were in similar, adjacent bottles on the shelf and, not being aware that there was creosote in the house, Parry accidentally gave it to his son. The inquest jury returned a verdict of 'death by misadventure'.

Sca Fell

It was customary at Christmas for climbing parties to assemble at Sca Fell (Scafell) in the Lake District and, in 1903, the fact that four tourists were killed while attempting to scale the peak in September did nothing to deter the climbers.

Shortly after midday on Christmas Day, experienced climbers Mr F. Botterill and Alexander Goodall left their party to attempt an ascent of the Sca Fell pinnacle. Having watched a superb sunset from the cairn at the top of the peak, they began to make their way back down via Deep Ghyll.

Ordinarily, Deep Ghyll should have been a rock climb but the ghyll was filled with snow and looked like a safe slope down which they could safely glissade, using an ice axe to check their progress and keep control of their pace. Twenty-six-year-old Goodall specifically asked to take the lead but almost as soon as he began the descent he overbalanced and fell flat on his back.

Sca Fell and Esk view, 1934. (Author's collection)

The Wastwater Hotel. (Author's collection)

He had driven his ice axe into the slope but was unable to hold onto it with his gloved hands and continued sliding down the slope, first on his back, then turning so that he was lying face-down and proceeding head first down the slope. He descended in this fashion for many hundreds of feet before he collided with the rocks at the base of Lord's Rake and died instantly.

It took Mr Botterill almost three hours to arrive at the same point, by which time other climbers had alerted rescuers, who stretchered Goodall's body to The Wastwater Hotel. An inquest on his death later determined that Goodall was 'accidentally killed'.

Liverpool

The Liverpool and Harrington Waterworks occupied an extensive range of buildings on Sussex Street, Water Street and Rock Street and, on the west side of the plant, was a large, brand new water tank, with a capacity of 250,000 gallons.

The construction of the tank was completed a few days before Christmas 1845 and by Christmas Day it was only about two-thirds full of water. Shortly after one o'clock in the afternoon, people living in Rock Street heard a terrible noise, which one resident described as '. . . like the roar of artillery.' Seconds later, something hit the houses with tremendous force. The tank had burst and a great surge of water washed through the street, knocking down walls, smashing windows and sweeping furniture and people before it.

A woman named Catherine Gibson drowned as she drew beer in the cellar of a public house, while Ann Smith and her baby Sarah Eliza were buried beneath a collapsed wall. John Devaney and another woman, coincidentally also named Catherine Gibson, brought the death toll to five, with many more people injured, mainly suffering from fractured bones.

An inquest on the five deaths concluded that the bursting of the tank was an unforeseeable catastrophe and a verdict of 'accidental death' was returned on all five victims. In January 1846, twenty-four-year-old Ann Devaney succumbed to her injuries and became the sixth fatality.

Blackburn

On Christmas Eve 1896, twenty-nine-year-old John Patrick Cunningham was attending a Christmas party at his sister's home in Blackburn, Lancashire. The drink was flowing freely and soon Cunningham became so drunk and quarrelsome that he was asked to leave. As he did so, he petulantly smashed his fist through a window and walked off.

On Christmas morning, Cunningham was found dead just behind his own house, a trail of blood leading from there to his sister's home. His death was due to blood loss from a severed artery, near the elbow of his right arm, caused by the broken window glass.

Liverpool

On Christmas Day 1919, two messengers found a dead body in an alley near Liverpool Town Hall. The battered and bloody woman was nude and her clothes, which lay nearby, looked to have been violently torn from her body. A number of coins were found nearby and, a little further down the street was a woman's purse, still containing money.

The woman was identified as fifty-two-year-old Elizabeth McDermott, a prostitute who was known locally by the street name of Bella Wilson. An arrest was quickly made but there was absolutely no evidence to connect sailor John Brien with Bella's murder and he was released. Another suspect was also arrested on suspicion of causing Bella's death, a bloodstained Irishman

Castle Street and Town Hall, Liverpool. (Author's collection)

who was seen staggering into the toilets at Lime Street Station on Christmas morning, with wounds on his head and face. However, he too was released due to lack of evidence and the inquest on Bella's death concluded on 12 January with a verdict of 'wilful murder against some person or persons unknown.'

The murder was never solved.

Halliwell, near Bolton

Henry Rostron from Halliwell was very fond of shooting and habitually carried a walking-stick gun in order to shoot sparrows. On Christmas Day 1860, he was about to go out shooting and had loaded his gun, when someone came to see him about a horse. He placed his gun on a chest of drawers in the kitchen and went out.

On Boxing Day his eighteen-year-old nephew Thomas came to visit and, picking up the gun, began to play with it. Mrs Rostron immediately told him to put it down as it was loaded, which he did. However, the following day, Thomas Ellam visited the house again.

While he was there, Mrs Rostron popped out to a nearby shop, leaving her nephew in charge of his two young cousins, one of whom was a baby in a cradle. The other was four-year-old Mary Elizabeth Rostron, known as Polly. As soon as Mrs Rostron left, Thomas began fiddling with the gun. It went off, shooting Polly and blowing off the entire top of her head, killing her instantly.

An inquest on Polly's death heard that Thomas, who was obviously distraught at what had happened, bore an excellent character and was a favourite nephew of the Rostrons. The inquest jury returned a verdict of 'accidental death' and, perhaps fortunately since he had been previously warned about touching the gun, Thomas faced no charges in respect of his cousin's tragic death.

Rochdale

At about half-past eight on Christmas morning 1855, thirteen-year-old Mary Birchenough, aka Mellor, was sliding on ice at Mr Threlfall's Mill at Sudden Brow near Rochdale, Lancashire. Against the advice of the boys who were sliding with her, Mary ventured too far out on the ice, which broke, plunging her into the freezing cold water. Although her companions immediately ran for help, it was more than half an hour before her body was recovered and all attempts at resuscitation proved fruitless.

Thornley, Preston

Twenty-year-old farm labourer Thomas Rhodes and his widowed mother, Isabella, were invited to spend Christmas Day 1929 with friends at a farm in Thornley, Lancashire. While Mrs Rhodes elected to go by bus, Thomas decided to cycle.

After an enjoyable day, mother and son left their friend's farmhouse separately, Thomas to cycle home and his mother to catch the 10.10 p.m. bus. She was escorted across the fields by her friends, who left her on the lane just a few yards from the bus stop.

Meanwhile, Thomas was having problems with his acetylene bicycle lamp, which was suddenly flaring up and dying down in the wind. As he freewheeled down a hill, his lamp dimmed and when it came on again, he was horrified to see a person walking along the lane only a yard in front of his bicycle.

Thomas tried to take avoiding action, swerving to the right but the pedestrian stepped the same way and Thomas hit her. He was thrown from his bicycle but quickly picked himself up and went to the woman – only then did Thomas realise that he had run over his own mother.

Thomas ran to the nearest farm for help and fifty-three-year-old Isabella was taken to the Preston Infirmary, where she died the following morning. The lane had no pavement and Mrs Rhodes was wearing dark clothes and walking with her back towards the oncoming traffic. Hence the inquest on her death exonerated Thomas from all blame for the tragic demise of his mother, which was deemed an 'accidental death' by the jury.

Droylsden

Mary Hanmer (or Hammer) and Timothy Faherty were both factory workers who originated from Ireland. For a while, they shared lodgings in Droylsden, near Manchester and were courting until Mary broke off the relationship on account of Timothy's fondness for drinking. Timothy moved to a different lodging house, although he remained on friendly terms with Mary and often called in to see her.

On Christmas Eve 1867, he asked her if she would go to church with him on Christmas Day and, although Mary refused, she was polite and pleasant, almost playful, in doing so.

On Christmas Day, Faherty called to see Mary to tell her that he was going back to Ireland and ask her if she had any messages. 'Give my respects to the green fields and the shamrock,' she replied. Minutes later, as Mary was washing some pots in the kitchen, other people in the house heard her say to Faherty, 'Get off with you, why have you come in here after me?' and seconds later, she screamed.

Bridget Broderick was asleep in her bedroom when Mary burst into the room, her face smeared with blood. Faherty was hot on her heels, wielding a poker and shouting, 'I'll kill you! I'll kill you!' at the top of his voice. Bridget watched in horror as Faherty hit Mary five times on the top of her head with the poker. Mary fell to the floor and said, 'Bridget, I am killed,' which were her last words. When Faherty dropped the poker, Bridget seized the chance to flee, fainting into the arms of neighbour Thomas Brown, who had come to see what the screaming was.

'Brown, I've killed her,' Faherty told him, cradling Mary in his arms and trying unsuccessfully to give her some water.

Somebody went for the police and, while waiting for them to arrive, Faherty sorrowfully told Brown that he loved Mary and would die for her.

He was tried at the Manchester Assize Court in March 1868, where Mr Justice Lush stated that he had rarely seen a clearer case of murder. The jury agreed, not needing to deliberate before finding Faherty guilty. He was executed on 4 April.

Prestwich

Edith Jane Birch worked as a kitchen maid at Prestwich, Lancashire, and was known to have a problem with sleepwalking. From childhood, her bedroom door was always locked from the outside when she retired to bed but even so, she was occasionally found wandering about outside, having dressed herself and escaped from her room.

Shortly before Christmas 1896, Edith spent the evening writing Christmas cards before going to bed. When her fellow servants came downstairs the next morning, it was evident that Edith was not yet up and about since none of the early morning jobs had been done. Her fully clothed body was found later that day in the River Irwell at Agecroft Bridge.

An inquest was held by coroner Mr J.F. Price and although it was clear that Edith had died through drowning, there was no evidence whatsoever to show how, when or why she came to be in the river. It was assumed that she had fallen in while sleepwalking but with no definite proof, the inquest jury returned an open verdict.

Bolton

By 1893, James and Margaret McDerby of Bolton had been married for twelve years and had produced six children. Unfortunately, Margaret was addicted to drink, which caused countless violent arguments between the couple, especially after she was sent to gaol for a month for neglecting her children.

After an argument on 23 December, James knocked his wife down and kicked her in the stomach as she lay on the floor. Bleeding heavily, Margaret struggled to her feet and staggered to a neighbour's house, where she fainted as soon as the door was opened and died within minutes from loss of blood.

Charged with her murder, McDerby was distraught. 'Yes, I did kick her,' he admitted, adding, 'I never kicked her in my life before. I never expected anything of this sort; God knows I did not.'

Thirty-eight-year-old McDerby appeared at the Manchester Assizes on 22 February 1894, where he agreed to plead guilty to manslaughter. However, when his defence counsel addressed the court on his client's behalf, a tragic story emerged. McDerby was a former member of the Royal Irish Constabulary (RIC) but was forced to forego promotion and eventually resign because of his wife's scandalous conduct. Nevertheless, he received a pension of 10s a week from the RIC as well as the money he earned in his regular job as a bill poster.

Margaret McDerby spent every penny of her housekeeping money on drink and, according to her children, would often pawn the blankets and their clothes to satisfy her cravings.

Margaret died on a Saturday, having been blind drunk for four whole days. James was out bill-posting all day in the freezing rain

Manchester Assize Courts, 1900s. (Author's collection)

and was cold and soaked to the skin. When he got home, there was no fire because Margaret had drunk the money he gave her for coal and there was no hot meal ready because she had spent the grocery money on rum and beer. However, the final straw for James was learning that Margaret had pawned his only shirt, leaving him with no dry clothes to change in to. At that point, James lost his temper and kicked his wife.

The life led by James and the couple's children was described in court as 'a perfect hell on earth' and presiding judge Mr Justice Charles obviously had a lot of sympathy for McDerby, who informed the judge that no punishment the law could inflict would be equal to the remorse he felt over his wife's death. He was sentenced to six months' imprisonment with hard labour.

Manchester

The deaths of Mary Jane Dyer and Margaret McCabe, who died in Crumpsall Workhouse on Christmas Day 1900, were initially attributed to peripheral neuritis, caused by arsenic in beer. Although there was ultimately some question about the cause of McCabe's death, at least thirteen deaths supposedly from the same cause were reported from Salford. Further cases were recorded at Liverpool, Crewe and Preston, where out of twelve samples of beer taken from different firms in the town, two were found to contain small quantities of arsenic and one contained what were described as 'serious amounts' of the poison.

Fulwood, near Preston

Fifty-two-year-old tramp John Taylor, who had only one leg, was well known in the Preston area and on 23 December 1876, he went to the police station to request a ticket for accommodation at the Fulwood Workhouse. However, once he arrived at the Workhouse, he was found to have 2s 2d in coins in his pocket. This meant that he was not a destitute person and therefore did not qualify for a bed and he was immediately turned out.

Unable to find lodgings, Taylor was seen at three o'clock on the morning of Christmas Eve by a policeman on the beat in Preston, who related that he was then '. . . shivering and shuddering from

head to foot' from the cold. At daybreak, Taylor was found lying helpless on the pavement, complaining of feeling poorly.

Only then was he taken to the infirmary at Fulwood Workhouse but it was too late and Taylor died from exposure on Christmas Day.

Liverpool ❦❦❦

On Christmas night 1879, Patrick Gibbons was holding a Christmas party at his home in Midghall Street, at which many of the guests were young people. Among them was Patrick's eighteen-year-old nephew, Patrick Kelly, who took exception when his uncle decided that it was time for the party to end. There was an argument between uncle and nephew, which became a physical fight and Kelly pulled out a knife and cut his uncle's face before storming out of the house.

He was followed by his sixteen-year-old cousin, Bridget Gibbons, who ran up the street after him and slapped his face. Kelly was seen to raise his hand and immediately afterwards Bridget collapsed, bleeding from a large wound in the side of her neck. Patrick fled and, when Bridget died, he was later found hiding under the mattress on his bed and arrested.

He was tried at the Liverpool Assizes in February 1880, where he denied stabbing his cousin. He admitted hitting her with his fist while he was holding a pipe in his hand, claiming that the pipe stem must have caused her injury. Kelly denied having had a knife and, indeed, none was ever found.

His defence counsel argued for a reduction in the charge from murder to manslaughter, saying that Patrick was walking away when his cousin hit him and provoked him into retaliating, which he did in hot blood with no intention of killing her.

The inquest jury agreed, finding Kelly guilty of manslaughter only. Presiding Judge Lord Chief Justice Coleridge seemed to disagree with the verdict, especially as the medical evidence clearly showed that Bridget's deep stab wound could not possibly have been inflicted with a pipe stem. Saying that the crime was '. . . just short of murder' Coleridge sentenced Kelly to twenty years' penal servitude.

Hawes Junction

On Christmas Eve 1910, the railways were busier than normal as people went home to be with their families. At Hawes Junction in Cumbria (then Westmorland) signalman Albert Sutton was nearing the end of a busy shift. His relief had just arrived when Sutton made a terrible mistake. Having signalled two light engines coupled together to proceed on the line towards Carlisle, he mistakenly allowed the London to Glasgow express train onto the same line. Since it was a fast train, a collision with the slower moving trains was inevitable and almost the first words Sutton spoke to his relief were, 'Go to Bunce [the stationmaster] and tell him that I am afraid I have wrecked the Scotch Express.'

The express was indeed wrecked. It ploughed into the slower trains at top speed and was derailed, the wooden carriages over-riding each other. As the gas pipes lighting the carriages fractured, fires broke out and spread through the train. Twelve people lost their lives in the incident, some crushed and others burned to death and a further seventeen people were injured.

Pemberton, Wigan

Mrs Gwendoline Florence Wiswall was getting her children ready to go to a Christmas party in 1945. Six-year-old Gwyneth and three-year-old Frederick John were in the bath together at the family home in Pemberton, Lancashire, when their mother momentarily left them alone while she went to their bedroom to fetch clean vests for them. When she returned to the bathroom an electric fire that had been standing on the edge of the bath had fallen into the water and the two children were unconscious.

Their mother tried to snatch the fire out of the water but received a severe electric shock herself and only then thought to unplug it. However, it was too late to save the children, who were electrocuted.

At the subsequent inquest, the jury returned two verdicts of 'accidental death' and the coroner stated that while he was entirely satisfied that Mrs Wiswall was a devoted mother, he felt duty bound to condemn the siting of any electrical appliances in a bathroom.

Liverpool

On Christmas Eve 1892, the occupants of a house on Bown Street gathered for a Christmas party. The gathering – which was described in the contemporary newspapers as 'a debauch' – started in the afternoon and continued until the early hours of Christmas morning.

Margaret Brannigan left the party drunk at about ten o'clock. Her husband Peter followed her upstairs to their apartment about an hour later and, according to a neighbour, Thomas Quinn, he ordered his wife to get up and light the fire.

'I can't, Peter, I am not able,' replied Margaret.

'If you don't get up, I'll throw you downstairs,' threatened Peter.

There followed a series of thuds and thumps, punctuated by cries and moans of pain but although it was obvious that Margaret was being beaten, neither Mr Quinn nor any other of the occupants of the house tried to help her.

The noises continued on an off until nine o'clock on Christmas morning, when Peter approached a neighbour asking if he might have a cup of tea for his wife, adding that she was nearly dead. The police and a doctor were called and found Margaret Brannigan's body lying naked on the heap of straw that served as her bed in her filthy rooms, her head and face bloody and bruised. A post-mortem examination revealed a number of old scars and bruises, as well as two recent black eyes. Her nose was broken, she had several deep cuts on her face and injuries to her shoulders, collar bones, arms, knees and thighs.

Dr Kellet-Smith found it difficult to determine the precise cause of Margaret's death, since none of her wounds were fatal. However, Smith believed that she had died from a combination of shock and exposure – the shock resulting from a severe beating and exposure caused by a night spent naked in bitterly cold weather. To further complicate matters, Margaret was addicted to drink and her death could possibly have been due to her excessive intake of alcohol.

When forty-year-old Brannigan appeared before Mr Justice Wills at the Liverpool Assizes, he insisted that he led a dog's life at home on account of his wife's heavy drinking. In view of the

Mr Justice Wills. (Author's collection)

fact that Margaret Brannigan's injuries could conceivably have been caused by drunken falls, the jury found her husband guilty of the lesser offence of manslaughter and he was sentenced to penal servitude for fourteen years.

Burnley

Behind the Tim Bobbin Inn at Burnley, Lancashire was a triangular disused quarry, known locally as Tim Bobbin Delph. Over Christmas 1887, the Delph froze over and on Boxing Day twelve-year-olds Frank Hartley and Thomas Hewitson were the first to venture onto the ice. After a little tentative sliding, Hewitson decided to test the strength of the ice by jumping on it but the ice broke and he went into the water. Hartley went to his rescue but he too fell in.

Fourteen-year-old Michael Davenport saw the boys in trouble and ran to a nearby house, where the people attending a Christmas party were about to start tea. Brothers Ezra and Joseph Tattersall, aged nineteen and seventeen respectively, brothers Joseph and John Barrett, aged forty-four and forty-three, and Joseph's nineteen-year-old son Arthur immediately ran down to the quarry to help. According to witnesses, the five would-be rescuers seemed to be panic stricken, dashing into the water without thinking and soon, all five were in need of rescuing themselves.

By now, ropes and ladders had been organised and Hartley and Hewitson were pulled from the water cold but alive. The efforts of the rescuers then turned to the five men from the Christmas party, none of whom were able to swim.

Ropes were thrown to the men but they were too cold to grasp them. John Barrett and Joseph Tattersall had at least tied ropes around their bodies before plunging into the water but since nobody was holding the other ends, this proved useless as a safety precaution.

In full view of a large crowd of people gathered on the quarry banks, who were trying every possible means of rescuing the men, they gradually sank beneath the water and did not resurface. Eventually, people cobbled together a makeshift raft and one by one the bodies of the five men were recovered using grappling irons and returned to the house where, just hours earlier, the Christmas rejoicing was in full swing.

Macclesfield

By 1880, William Stanway and Ann Mellor had lived together as man and wife for ten years. The couple earned a living as hawkers, sometimes working together, sometimes separately, but at Christmas they were expecting to meet at the house in Macclesfield, Cheshire, where Ann was staying.

William arrived home at eight o'clock on the morning of Christmas Day and he, Ann and a friend immediately went out for a drink and continued drinking on and off all day. When he arrived home, William gave Ann all his money – a sovereign and a few coppers. Thus, when he got hungry, he was furious that she hadn't bought any food and began to beat and kick her. His behaviour towards her was so violent that it drew a crowd of around 200 people, not one of whom tried to intervene to end her suffering. Ann managed to escape and ran into a house but William followed her and dragged her out until eventually he tired of beating her and walked away, leaving Ann to crawl home and get into bed.

An hour later, William arrived back at their lodgings. He and Ann had previously adopted a little girl, Sarah Ann Blunt, who was later to say that William shouted for Ann and, when he was told that she was in bed, ordered her to come downstairs or he would come up to her with a red hot poker.

Ann came down wearing just a chemise and a petticoat and, in front of their adopted daughter, William ran the red hot poker through his wife's belly. Ann promptly fainted and when she came to, she took a few sips of water then went to a friend's house, where she stayed the night. She complained that William had burned her, showing her friend a seared mark on her stomach and spent an uncomfortable night, during which she vomited several times but she refused to seek medical attention as she didn't want William to be arrested.

Ann walked home at six o'clock on the morning of Boxing Day, where she found William still drinking. 'I nearly spoiled my wife with a poker last night,' he said to a friend. When he realised the full extent of the damage he had done to Ann, William pleaded with her to see a doctor but she flatly refused. By the time she could be persuaded, it was too late for any medical help and Ann died in William's arms on 27 December, just before the doctor arrived.

William was charged with wilful murder and appeared at the Chester Assizes on 2 February 1881. His defence counsel tried to argue that William's drunkenness at the time was sufficient grounds to reduce the crime from murder to manslaughter. The jury disagreed and found William guilty.

Sentenced to death, he fell to his knees and sobbed, pleading for mercy and saying that he did not know that he had done it. His grovelling counted for nothing and he was executed on 21 February 1881.

Clifton Junction

On 27 December 1881, James Thornley of Clifton was travelling home from Manchester by train. There was a very dense fog at the time.

The train stopped and, thinking that it had arrived at the station, Thornley disembarked. Unfortunately, the train had stopped about 100 yards from the station on the bridge over the Bury, Bolton and Manchester Canal. When Thornley stepped out of the train, he also stepped off the bridge, falling 100 feet into the water below. His body was later discovered head down in the mud and silt on the canal bottom. In reporting the accident, the contemporary newspapers recalled another nearly identical tragedy at precisely the same spot, almost six years earlier to the day.

Lytham St Annes

On Christmas Eve 1919, a woman's body was found in sand dunes near Lytham St Annes, Lancashire. She had been shot three times. Close by, the police found her hat, umbrella and a pair of man's kid gloves, heavily stained with blood and, four days later, some children playing in the dunes dug up a Webley revolver that had recently been fired. The woman was identified by her sister as twenty-five-year-old Kathleen Elsie Breaks, who was usually known as Kitty. The dead woman was married but had been separated from her husband for almost eighteen months and, at the time of her death, was courting Frederick Rothwell Holt, a former Lieutenant, who was invalided out of the Army during the First World War, suffering from amnesia and depression.

Ownership of the gloves and the revolver was traced to Holt, who was arrested but seemed unable to comprehend why he had been apprehended. He was tried for wilful murder at the Assizes in Manchester in February 1920, where his defence counsel tried to establish that he was unfit to plead. A special jury was sworn to determine his fitness to stand trial, which went ahead in spite of the defence counsel's concerns.

There was no doubt that Holt suffered from some form of mental illness. He went through the entire trial gazing blankly into space and at one stage was seen ardently reading a newspaper, which he was holding upside down. He imagined that the police were sending dogs and germ-covered flies into his prison cell in order to hurt him. Nevertheless, the prosecution believed that Holt murdered Kitty knowing that she had recently made a will in his favour to get his hands on her £5,000 life assurance policy.

At the trial, Holt's father, stepmother and sister all swore that he was in bed by 10.10 p.m. on the night of the murder. If this were true, it would have been impossible for Holt to have killed Kitty, who was seen leaving a hotel at 9 p.m., but the jury found Holt guilty and he was sentenced to death.

Holt's defence counsel appealed the sentence on the grounds that he had contracted syphilis in Malaysia, which could have affected his mental state. In addition, Holt had a family history of insanity, his grandfather and a first cousin both having been declared insane. In the face of this new evidence, the Home Secretary ordered a medical inquiry into Holt's state of mind but ultimately decided that there were no grounds to interfere with the sentence and Holt was hanged by John Ellis at Manchester's Strangeways Prison on 13 April 1920.

Frodsham, near Chester

On Christmas Day 1821, the Guest family of Frodsham, Cheshire sat down to a Christmas dinner of roast beef, which was accompanied by freshly made horseradish sauce. Tragically, instead of horseradish, the family servant had accidentally gathered roots of deadly poisonous wolf's bane.

Almost immediately after eating the sauce, Mrs Guest began to feel nauseous. Her pulse slowed, her heartbeat became irregular and her breathing became more and more torturous until she died. Her husband and children had eaten less of the highly toxic root and, although they were very ill and their lives were initially despaired of, they eventually recovered.

Liverpool

It was customary for the staff at the Workhouse Infirmary in Liverpool to put on some form of Christmas entertainment for the patients and in 1897 it was decide to stage an exhibition of living waxworks.

While rehearsing, twenty-five-year-old nurse Edith Ellen Ashcroft got too close to the hot footlights. Her long, muslin costume accidentally brushed against them and it immediately burst into flames.

Nurse Ashcroft was very badly burned and died within hours of the incident. An inquest was held on 28 December, at which a verdict of 'accidental death' was returned.

Barrow-in-Furness

Joseph Baines and his wife Ellen from Barrow-in-Furness, Cumbria, had been quarrelling for several days. Until 1881, Baines was a hard-working, relatively successful businessman but when he inherited the sum of £500, he began drinking heavily and had soon spent all of his money. It was left to his wife to support the couple and their seven children, which she did by selling fish in the market.

Her husband became a violent, drunken bully, and would happily have spent every penny of her earnings on drink. Time and time again, Ellen tried to leave him but he simply wouldn't allow her to do so.

The couple quarrelled incessantly in the few days prior to Christmas 1885 because Ellen refused to give Joseph money for drink. On Christmas morning, Ellen went to her neighbour's house to enquire what the time was and her husband followed her there and, in front of the horrified neighbours, pulled out a knife and stabbed her four times in the chest and abdomen. He was subdued by the man of the house and, when taken to the police station, calmly asked, 'Is she dead yet?' adding, 'If not, she ought to be.'

Having killed his wife in front of witnesses and then, having made a full confession to the police that he did so deliberately, Joseph Baines's trial for wilful murder at the Assizes was little more than a formality. It took the jury just seven minutes to find him guilty and he was executed on 9 February 1886. Although he showed no remorse for the brutal killing, he did ask the chaplain to make it known that he regretted having said anything that reflected on his wife's honour.

Walton-le-Dale, Preston 🍃❅🍃

When Stephen Burke was hanged in 1865 for the wilful murder of his wife in Preston, there was nowhere for the couple's orphaned children to go other than the Workhouse. In 1867, seven-year-old Patrick Burke was an inmate of Walton-le-Dale Workhouse and, expecting visitors over the festive period, on 23 December the governor decided to wage war on lice and nits.

He obtained a pot of ointment from the surgery and slathered it over every boy's head, leaving it for nearly five hours before it was washed off. The following morning, more than eighty boys complained of feeling ill.

Four boys were particularly poorly, all complaining of exhaustion and excess salivation. Dr Smith was called to examine them and admitted all four to the House of Recovery at Preston, where Patrick Burke sadly died.

The doctor had no idea what had caused his death until he received an anonymous letter detailing the treatment of all the Workhouse boys with 'blue ointment' by the governor. When questioned, the governor explained how he had tried to rid the boys of infestation and produced some of the ointment he had used. When it was analysed, it was found to have high mercury content and Smith realised that Burke had been poisoned by absorbing mercury through his skin. Smith re-examined all of the other boys and found it necessary to confine forty of them to bed and medicate them.

At an inquest on Patrick's death held by coroner Mr Myres, it was pointed out that, but for the anonymous letter, nobody would have known what caused the child's death, neither would the other boys in the institution have received the necessary medical treatment. The inquest jury returned a verdict of 'accidental death' and although they asked the coroner to officially caution the governor about his future conduct, they recommended no legal action against him.

Liverpool 🍃❅🍃

Over Christmas 1892, an extraordinarily large number of sudden, violent deaths were reported to the Liverpool coroner.

On Christmas Day alone there were twenty-four cases including one alleged murder, six children suffocated or burned to death, and about the same number of old people found dead. The figures on Boxing Day were very similar and it was reported in the *Northern Echo* that preliminary investigations by the coroner's office suggested that alcohol was directly or indirectly responsible for the majority of cases.

Sale

Martin Burke returned to his home in Sale, Cheshire, on Christmas Day 1888, after an absence of eight years. At first, he and his father engaged in pleasant conversation but Martin had been drinking and was soon arguing and cursing his father, who ordered him out of the house.

Martin promptly knocked his father off his chair and kicked him unconscious with his pointed-toed clogs. When the police arrived, they found Martin in his shirt-sleeves, brandishing a pair of tongs. Inspector Meredith disarmed him and Martin promised to go quietly but as soon as he was handcuffed, he butted Meredith and kicked his shins, causing a severe laceration. Despite being handcuffed, Martin managed to knock Meredith and PC Green over and the three grappled on the floor for some time before the police finally tied Martin's legs together with a cord and carried him to Sale police station.

James Burke was left with two black eyes, a one-inch-long wound on his temple that penetrated to the bone, abrasions on his nose and cheek and severe bruising, while Meredith would need at least a week off work to recuperate from his injuries.

Martin Burke was tried at the Cheshire Assizes for unlawful wounding. He claimed to have been so drunk that he didn't know what he was doing and said that he was sorry that he had hurt his father. His drunkenness was not seen as a mitigating factor and he was sentenced to eight months' imprisonment.

TEN

NORTHERN IRELAND

Camlough

On the evening of Christmas Day 1867, James Quinn, John Smith and Henry and Bernard McQuade left their homes and went on a pub crawl in Camlough where, with the exception of Bernard, all drank copious quantities of whisky.

On their way home, an argument started between the men and Smith eventually left the group and went home. Later, he was working in the byre milking his cow, when Henry McQuade appeared and asked him what spite Smith had against him that he wished to have a row on the road.

Smith hit Henry with the milking stool, leaving him with a badly cut eye. Henry was taken into Smith's house, where his wound was attended to, while Bernard went to the byre to remonstrate with Smith.

Bernard retreated after the milking stool was thrown at him, hitting him hard on the shoulder. Now Quinn went to the byre and began to harangue Smith, who picked up a shovel and told him, 'I'll end your days.' With that, he hit Quinn hard, knocking him senseless.

Twenty-two-year-old Quinn was taken into Smith's house and, as soon as he had recovered sufficiently, he was helped to his own home, where he died on 27 December. An inquest held by coroner Mr J.M. Magee returned a verdict of manslaughter against Smith, who fled the area shortly after hitting Quinn and had not been seen since. He was believed to have travelled to America and does not appear to have returned to County Armagh to stand trial.

Dungate, near Cookstown

Maria and Elizabeth 'Lizzie' McGurk kept a public house at Dungate, approximately nine miles from Cookstown, County Tyrone. The pub was very strictly run, and the sisters normally closed at just after nine o'clock at night but on Christmas Eve 1898, the doors were locked slightly earlier than usual, probably because of the extra religious devotions demanded by the season.

The sisters shared their home with their brother, Michael, and a servant, Mr Loughran, and at five o'clock on Christmas morning, Michael, who slept downstairs, was roused by shouts of 'Fire!' He ran up to his sisters' room and saw flames coming from beneath the door of a spare room opposite their bedroom.

The room had not been used for eight weeks. Michael shouldered open the locked door to see if he could extinguish the fire but was beaten back by the fierceness of the conflagration. He sent Lizzie to a neighbour for help and, when she returned, she helped him and Loughran to ferry buckets of water from the river to the house. Nobody had seen Maria McGurk since the outbreak of the fire but Loughran was later to say that he heard Lizzie telling her to go back upstairs. The flames spread with astonishing speed and in only a few minutes the roof caved in.

When the fire was finally out, Maria and Lizzie were found dead in the smouldering remains of their home. At an inquest held by coroner Mr John Malone, the jury were told that there was nothing to suggest what caused the fire. Since Maria and Lizzie were known to have escaped the blaze, it was theorised that they went back into the house to try and retrieve a box of valuable documents, mortgages and deeds, which was normally kept in their bedroom. The inquest returned verdicts of 'burned to death' on both sisters, adding that there was no evidence as to the cause of the fire.

Ballynagard

Four elderly spinster sisters named Quigley lived together in a house at Ballynagard near Londonderry. On Christmas morning 1926, a fifth sister, who worked as a housekeeper for an elderly uncle living nearby, joined them for breakfast.

The sisters and their manservant, Frank Doherty, drank tea and ate bread, butter and forcemeat – a finely ground meat mixed with spices. Doherty felt sick almost immediately after eating but recovered after a tot of brandy, while the sisters were well enough to eat their Christmas dinner of duck, potatoes, more forcemeat and a corn flour pudding.

On Boxing Day, the sisters went to visit an elderly aunt and, during the visit, one of them felt terribly ill. Another sister took her home, while the two remaining sisters stayed overnight with their aunt, returning home on 27 December.

They promised their aunt that they would return that evening and when they didn't, the old lady fretted until 30 December then sent a messenger to check on her nieces. The servant found all four sisters ill in bed, being cared for after a fashion by Doherty, who periodically gave them hot milk. The messenger took it upon himself to visit a chemist at Derry for a bottle of medicine but on 31 December, one of the sisters suffered convulsions.

Only then was a doctor called and on his arrival, he found Rose dead and Kate dying from ptomaine poisoning, probably from the forcemeat. A third sister, Sarah Anne, died the following morning, while Maggie was expected to recover, as did Mary, the housekeeper for their uncle.

Tragically, when the news of Rose's death was broken to her aunt, Sarah collapsed and died from shock.

Larne Lough

On 21 December 1871, chief officer John Sowden and four of his men from Portmuck Coastguard Station travelled to Larne by boat to do some Christmas shopping. They were accompanied by Sowden's twelve-year-old son, who was also named John.

Having done their shopping, they left Larne harbour at about half-past three in the afternoon for the return journey, raising

Larne, 1916. (Author's collection)

the boat's sails when they reached open water. Soon afterwards, people on the shore heard cries for help.

A boat was immediately launched and the coastguards' vessel was found off Islandmagee, drifting towards Ballygally Head. Edward Jeffers and Benjamin Brooks were still on board, although both were insensible and there was no sign of the other occupants.

Jeffers and Brooks were taken ashore, although Brooks died before reaching dry land. Jeffers was suffering from the effects of exposure, although he was well enough to appear at the inquest on Brooks' death a few days later, by which time, the body of John Sowden senior had also been recovered.

Jeffers told coroner Alexander Markham that all the men had been perfectly sober when they set out on the return journey to Portmuck. When a sudden squall capsized the boat shortly after her sails were raised, he and Brooks managed to cling to the side of the boat and succeeded in righting her but she immediately capsized again and settled on her side. They were fast drifting towards Ballygally Head when they were rescued.

The inquest returned a verdict of accidentally drowned on both Brooks and John Sowden and, at the time of the inquest,

Ballygally Head. (Author's collection)

John Sowden junior and two men named Laycock and Powell remained missing, presumed drowned.

Near Antrim

The Cookstown to Belfast train left Antrim Station on Boxing Day 1876 and had travelled only about a mile when it collided with a mineral train travelling in the opposite direction on the single-track line. Both trains were proceeding at full speed and it was classed as a miracle that there was only one fatality.

Although several people were injured, the only person to die in the accident was Matilda Lowry, the wife of an Antrim jeweller, who sustained a fractured skull and severe facial injuries. (Both of Mrs Lowry's children were seriously hurt in the crash but are believed to have survived.)

An inquest on Mrs Lowry's death heard that a bell was always rung before trains left Antrim Station to authorise them to proceed. The only person with the authority to ring the bell was stationmaster Andrew McKillop but the inquest was told that, because McKillop was busy, telegraph boy James Delaney took it upon himself to act on his behalf.

The bell should not have been rung until the mineral train had passed through the station, hence the inquest jury found that Mrs Lowry's death was caused by the negligence of the station staff and returned verdicts of manslaughter against McKillop and the driver and guard of the Cookstown to Belfast train, John Macrory and John Malcolmson.

All three appeared at the Antrim Assizes on 10 March 1877, where it was pointed out by McKillop's defence counsel that the person who should have been in the dock was Delaney, who rang the bell without the proper authorisation to do so. All three men were found not guilty and discharged.

Note: Some publications name the train guard as John Turner rather than John Malcolmson.

Derrygonnelly

Poor Law Guardian John Saunderson Trotter was at home in Derrygonnelly with his family on Christmas Eve 1898 when he suddenly seemed to go insane. He snatched up a loaded revolver and ran out of his house, saying that he would shoot the first person he met.

That unlucky young man was twenty-four-year-old John Dolan, a complete stranger to Trotter, who was innocently walking down the road when Trotter rushed up and shot him in the eye. He died instantly and Trotter briefly bent over him before rushing into some offices, all the while waving his revolver about and repeating, 'He must be shot, he must be shot!'

Trotter was arrested and taken before magistrates but seemed to have absolutely no idea of what was happening and fell down several times in the dock. Doctors were satisfied that he was insane and, although he was committed for trial at the next Fermanagh Assizes, he was sent to Omagh Asylum rather than Enniskillen Gaol. His trial in March 1899 was brief – he was found guilty but insane and sentenced to be detained in Dundrun Asylum until Her Majesty's pleasure be known.

Note: Some publications state that the shooting occurred on Boxing Day.

Belfast

Joseph Macauley was a hatter and bandbox manufacturer, who had premises on Church Street, Belfast and on Christmas Eve 1867, he returned from the Corn Exchange, where he was playing the violoncello at a dancing class, to find his shop on fire. As soon as the fire was first observed, neighbours leaped into action but they were so focused on trying to get people out of the house that nobody thought to notify the fire brigade for almost thirty minutes.

Once they were made aware of the emergency, the fire brigade were very quickly on the scene. The Macauley family lived over the shop and Joseph knew that his wife and four daughters were probably trapped upstairs but firemen prevented him from entering the property and would not let him climb the ladder that had been put up to the windows. He was told that two of his daughters had been taken to a neighbour's house but sadly five-year-old Harriet was near death and died soon afterwards. Mrs Harriet Macauley senior was lowered by rope from a kitchen on the third storey but died within minutes of reaching the General Hospital.

When the inquest was held, two more of Macauley's daughters had died. Fourteen-year-old Maggie (Margaret) and eighteen-

Belfast from City Hall. (Author's collection)

month-old Sarah both perished in the blaze, although, at the time the inquest was reported, six-year-old Jane was still clinging precariously to life. Two firemen were also injured while attempting to rescue the girls but were said to be recuperating at home.

Macauley told the inquest that he had forty dozen gross of bandboxes stored in the shop, which would have been highly inflammable and that the boxes he made earlier on the day of the fire would be drying out around the stove.

In returning verdicts that the deceased died from 'accidental burning and suffocation', the inquest jury recommended that the city should have a permanent fire brigade and that more portable fire escapes should be provided.

Ballymena

Nineteen-year-old William Kilpatrick was a soldier in the Royal Irish Rifles, stationed at Belfast, and, in mid-December 1894, he told his brother John that he would be home for Christmas. However, there was no sign of him and on Christmas morning John heard that a soldier had been drowned in the River Maine, County Antrim. Suspecting that the drowned man might be his brother, John and another brother, James, went down to the river, with a friend, John Craig. There they found a pile of clothing on the bank, with a print made by a bare foot near the river.

'This is Willie's – Willie must be drowned,' John said on seeing the clothes and immediately went back home to tell his parents, leaving James by the riverside.

There were people gathered on both banks of the river and James asked one man, William Jackson, to show him where the body was. Jackson led James to the point on the bank opposite, on which Willie's body lay and, before anyone could stop him, James waded into the river with the intention of retrieving his brother's body.

When he was about halfway across the river, he suddenly got out of his depth and began to sink. He threw up his arms and shouted for help but not one of the onlookers was able to swim and they were forced to watch helplessly as James battled against the current for a few moments before disappearing beneath the surface of the water.

It was seven days before James's body was recovered and, in the meantime, an inquest had been held on the death of his brother, William. The only thing that could be established about William was that he was absent without leave from his unit and the inquest jury returned an open verdict that he was 'found drowned'. When coroner Alexander Caruth held an inquest on the death of the second Kilpatrick brother the jury's verdict was that twenty-one-year-old James was 'accidentally drowned'.

Lurgan

On Christmas Eve 1895, Ellen Falcon and her husband left their home in Balteagh for a shopping trip in Lurgan, County Armagh. While there, both Ellen and her husband had a few drinks and somehow became separated. Eventually, unable to find each other, both set off for home alone.

In the dark, Mr Falcon accidentally strayed off his path and stumbled into a quarry. Fortunately, a passer-by heard him shouting for help and found him standing in the water, which reached almost to his mouth. Falcon was extricated and taken to a nearby house, where he was dried out and allowed to stay until daylight.

Since Falcon was away from home until Christmas morning, nobody realised that Ellen Falcon had also failed to return from her shopping trip. Her body was found in a ditch between Lurgan and her home and, at the inquest on her death before coroner Mr W.H. Atkinson, it was conjectured that, having fallen into the ditch, she was too drunk to get out again. Dr Agnew stated that Ellen Falcon died from exposure on the night of 24/25 December and the inquest jury returned a verdict in accordance with the medical evidence.

Tullynacross

Sixteen-year-old Hugh Bassett of Downpatrick was spending Christmas Day 1862 with his grandparents in Tullynacross, County Antrim. At about four o'clock in the afternoon, he

decided to go out with a gun to shoot birds and within ten minutes he was dead, shot through the heart by his own gun.

From the position of his body, doctors deduced that in crossing a ditch separating two fields, the trigger had caught on a thorn or twig and an inquest held by coroner Mr John Ward settled on a verdict of 'accidental death'.

The *Belfast Newsletter* strongly condemned the practice of shooting on Christmas Day, saying that it too often led to fatalities and, in this case '. . . a most respectable family are plunged in the greatest grief and their Christmas joy and gladness turned into weeping and mourning.'

Islandmagee

On Boxing Day 1876, twelve-year-old Alexander McLernon of Islandmagee, County Antrim, went to visit his married sister, Mrs Hoy, who was unwell. When he got there, he found everyone too busy caring for the invalid to pay much attention to him.

He amused himself for a while playing with a small child, but then found a bottle of whisky in the kitchen and helped himself to several drinks.

Alexander left his sister's house at between three and four o'clock and although she lived only about a quarter of a mile from her father's house, he never arrived home. Alexander's father assumed that he was spending the night with his sister, while she believed he had gone home, so nobody even realised that he was missing. However, on the following day, somebody looking out of a window at Mrs Hoy's house saw something unusual lying in a nearby field and a closer inspection revealed that it was Alexander's body. Doctors determined that the child had passed out due to intoxication and died from exposure to the cold.

Tullyvallen

On 27 December 1891, farmer James Murphy was found dead on a pile of turf in his kitchen at Tullyvallen, County Armagh. Murphy lived with his sister, Anne, and both were well known in the locality for their miserly habits.

The cause of Murphy's death was determined to be pneumonia, which was accelerated by self-neglect and malnourishment. Neither he nor his sister had eaten any food except milk for a long time and they ate nothing at all on Christmas Day. Murphy's death was made even stranger when his sister died the day after his demise, yet the farmer owned land and property worth more than £40,000 and had other assets that exceeded £7,000 in value.

Londonderry

In 1884, farmer John Deery was invited to a friend's house for his Christmas dinner. Nine people were sitting around the table eating roast beef with all the trimmings, when Deery was suddenly seen to go black in the face.

Without making a single sound, he slumped to the floor and died within a minute and a post-mortem examination later revealed that he had a large piece of beef lodged in his throat. An inquest later returned a verdict of 'death by suffocation'.

Belfast

John and Elizabeth Anne Quinn had lived together as man and wife for around twelve years, although they had only been legally wed for a couple of months. On Boxing Day 1877, both had been drinking and an argument began while they were eating their supper. Elizabeth's elderly mother, Ann Mooney, lived with the couple and the argument started when Elizabeth refused to give her mother anything to eat. John promptly shared his own food with his mother-in-law, which angered his wife, who snatched his cup and threw it against the fire grate.

'You scut, if you earned that as I have had to do you would not have thrown it against the grate,' John told his wife, who promptly threw her husband's plate into the fire, closely followed by a bottle of pickled cabbage.

Angered, John stood up and hit his wife twice with his fist on her breast. The first blow knocked her over and, when she got up, he hit her again. This time, she didn't fall but staggered against the wall for a moment before rushing to her front door, shouting 'Murder!' before collapsing on her doorstep as if dead.

High Street, Belfast. (Author's collection)

Neighbours carried her inside and placed her in front of the fire, barely alive. She died soon afterwards and Dr Charles Wadsworth, who made a post-mortem examination, could find no definitive cause of death. Apart from a black eye, there were no marks of violence on Elizabeth's body and her internal organs were apparently healthy, except for '. . . a slight congestion of the membranes of the brain.' It was Wadsworth's opinion that Elizabeth Quinn died from nervous shock.

The inquest jury found a verdict of manslaughter against John Quinn, although they qualified their verdict by adding that they believed that he had been much provoked.

Quinn stood trial for manslaughter in March 1878 but the trial jury shared the opinion of the inquest jury that Elizabeth had contributed towards her own demise. Since there were no marks of violence other than a black eye and, as Elizabeth was known to have been drunk at the time of her death, the jury found it impossible to decide if she died from her husband's blows or from injuries sustained by falling over while drunk. They gave Quinn the benefit of the doubt and he was acquitted.

ELEVEN

WALES

Cardiff

Nineteen-year-old Winifred Ellen Fort helped her father to run a lodging house for Greek sailors in Cardiff and, in 1916, she began a relationship with one of the residents. However, Alex Bakerlis was terribly jealous and flew into a rage every time Winifred even spoke to another man. His behaviour became so irrational that Winifred ended their relationship and her father gave Bakerlis notice to quit.

Winifred asked a friend to return a ring and some letters to Bakerlis but he refused to accept them, saying that he would only take them from Winifred herself. On the evening of Christmas Day 1916, Bakerlis approached his former girlfriend as she stood chatting to a friend on Bute Road. Winifred slipped the ring from her finger and gave it to him, telling him that she would go inside and fetch his letters, but, before she had a chance to do so, Bakerlis knocked her over and began to stab her frenziedly.

Minutes later, a policeman saw Bakerlis running towards him, still clutching a bloody knife. Bakerlis readily admitted to stabbing Winifred moments earlier and, when she died from blood poisoning on 28 December, he was charged with her wilful murder. Having been caught literally red-handed, he was found guilty at the Cardiff Assizes on 6 March 1917 and hanged on 10 April by John Ellis.

Penmaenmawr

John Thomas was employed in the granite sett quarries at Penmaenmawr in Caernarvonshire. On Christmas Eve 1878, he was kicking the snow from the wheels of a waggon that stood on an elevated tramway on the face of the rock when his feet suddenly slipped from under him and he fell backwards off the tramway.

Although other workers rushed to him, he fell over 40 feet and sustained such serious injuries that he was dead when they reached him. The coroner for Caernarvonshire, Mr J.H. Roberts, later recorded a verdict of 'accidental death'.

Holyhead

Gwenellen Jones was separated from her husband, Morris, and living with forty-nine-year-old William Murphy in Holyhead, Anglesey. However, high unemployment forced Murphy to leave the area to seek work and, while he was away, Gwen moved in with Robert Jones.

When Murphy returned to Holyhead, he called on Gwen's father to find out where she was. John Parry told him that he didn't know his daughter's whereabouts but Murphy was suspicious and told him that if he found Gwen with another man he would kill her.

On Christmas Day 1909, he carried out his threat. Gwen was drinking in a pub in the town with a woman friend when Murphy came in and asked to speak to her alone. Gwen left with him willingly but when Murphy returned alone some time later, his face was badly scratched and his handkerchief was blood-stained.

Murphy initially claimed to have been involved in a fight with two men but later admitted to killing Gwen by first strangling her, then cutting her throat and dragging her body by the hair into a drainage ditch, holding her head underwater to make absolutely sure that she was dead. He claimed that Gwen was drunk but that she had agreed to make love to him, saying that she was planning to leave Holyhead. Afterwards, Murphy realised that he couldn't bear the thought of Gwen with another man and so killed her.

Since Murphy had confessed, his trial at the Anglesey Assizes was a formality and his defence counsel's only hope was to convince the jury that Murphy was insane at the time of the murder. They were unable to do so and, after just three minutes' deliberation, the jury found him guilty. He was given the mandatory death sentence and was hanged at Caernarvon by Henry Pierrepoint on 15 February 1910.

Criccieth

On 27 December 1898, the police were contacted about the Williams family from Ivy Cottage, Criccieth. Neighbours believed that they were staying with relatives in Nottingham but when family members arrived to visit them, people realised that nobody had actually seen William Williams, his wife Ethel or their two sons since 8 December.

The cottage doors were locked and when PC Owen put a ladder up to the front bedroom window, he could see Williams lying on his back with a revolver on his chest. Owen and Reverend William Evans Jones, whose wife was Mrs Williams's aunt, forced an entry into the cottage.

Three-year-old Douglas Gordon Williams and his two-year-old brother Arthur had both died from single gunshot wounds behind their right ears. Twenty-four-year-old Ethel Williams had been shot twice in the head, while her husband had been shot through the roof of his mouth.

The inquest heard that, over the past three months, Williams had been behaving strangely and coroner Dr Hunter Hughes remarked that it was a pity that nobody had thought to mention that fact to the authorities. Although Williams was thought of as a quiet, rather morose man, who was never seen under the influence of alcohol outside his home, there were rumours that the former sailor went on drinking sprees, during which he would mistreat his wife. He was known to brandish a loaded revolver when drunk and a search of his cottage revealed a number of copies of *American Police News* magazine, which contained graphic descriptions and pictures of revolver tragedies. At the inquest on the four deaths, the coroner referred to these as

The Green, Criccieth. (Author's collection)

'pernicious literature', saying that they should never be allowed to be published for fear of falling into the hands of people like Williams, who were addicted to drink and subject to mental aberrations.

The inquest jury eventually returned a verdict of wilful murder against William Williams in respect of the deaths of his wife and sons, finding that he then committed suicide while temporarily insane.

Penrhyn Castle, Bangor

Every night at eleven o'clock, it was the duty of nineteen-year-old servant Charles Wilkins to close the gates of Penrhyn Castle, the home of The Honourable Douglas Pennant MP. However, on 23 December 1878 it had been snowing and Wilkins was unable to push the gate closed.

He used a lever to raise the heavy gate slightly but unfortunately he lifted it clean off its hinges and it fell on him. Since the gate weighed around ten hundredweight, Wilkins died instantaneously.

Coroner Mr Roberts held an inquest the following day, which recorded a verdict of 'accidental death'.

Wrexham

Sixty-one-year-old James Opie had lived with Sarah Martin at Wrexham for about three years when she left him for forty-three-year-old Thomas Grice. On 23 December 1893, Sarah and Grice were drinking in The Nag's Head in Wrexham when they were joined by Opie.

At first the conversation between the three was friendly but then Opie and Grice began to argue about Sarah until eventually, Opie pulled out a plaid handkerchief, in which something heavy was wrapped, and hit Grice over the head.

Grice staggered slightly but insisted, 'I'm not hurt,' and the other drinkers, who had detained Opie after the incident, let him go. Opie left the public house but soon afterwards, Sarah and Grice decided to move to another inn. They went out by the back door to try and avoid Opie but as they walked towards Ellesmere, he suddenly appeared out of nowhere and knocked Sarah down. Grice tried to defend her and the two men began scuffling, while Sarah fled in fear.

Opie followed her, leaving Grice lying on the ground. He was helped to his feet by a passer-by and managed to stagger home to his lodgings, where he was put to bed by his fellow lodgers, who were under the impression that he was simply drunk. At one o'clock in the afternoon of Christmas Eve, Grice died and a post-mortem examination revealed that his skull was fractured in several places.

Opie was arrested and, although he denied hitting Grice, insisting that the deceased attacked him first, the inquest jury returned a verdict of manslaughter against him. He was tried at the Denbighshire Assizes in January 1894, where the jury found him guilty but added a recommendation for mercy. Opie was sentenced to five years' imprisonment.

Porth, Rhondda Valley

As Mrs Catherine Bowen was walking down Bridge Street in Porth on 23 December 1894, the ground literally opened up beneath her and she suddenly disappeared from view. People rushed to the spot where she was last seen and found that a huge hole had appeared out of nowhere and there was no sign of Mrs Bowen.

A collier, Mr Jones, volunteered to be lowered into the hole to look for her but the rope snapped and he too vanished into the bowels of the earth. A third man eventually succeeded in rescuing both Mrs Bowen and Jones. Mrs Bowen was relatively unscathed but Jones died from his injuries the following day.

An inquest was told that the hole, which was 30 feet deep, was the result of subsidence into old mine workings and recorded a verdict of accidental death.

Pembroke

Finding themselves at a loose end on Christmas Day 1883, John Riley, George Ford, Morris Neil, William James and Thomas Lewis, who were all apprentices at the Pennar Works, hired a small boat and went out on the Pembroke River. As they neared Bentlass, the boat capsized and the five youths were thrown into the water.

Two managed to cling to the upturned boat and a third grabbed an oar, while a fourth swam to the bank and raised the alarm. However, seventeen-year-old George Ford sank without trace and, while his friends were rescued, George's body was not recovered until low tide, when it was found close to the spot where the capsize occurred. An inquest jury later determined that he was 'accidentally drowned'.

Pontypridd

On Christmas Day 1891, PC Rees Davies found the body of a man in the River Taff at Pontypridd. With the aid of his sergeant, he removed the corpse to the stables of The Bridge Inn, where it was identified as collier Moses Lewis from Ynysbwl. A post-mortem examination by Dr Howard Davies showed that Lewis had bruises on his forehead, elbows and the backs of both hands and a deep scratch on his nose, as well as a Y-shaped wound on his right temple. When Davies examined the wound more closely, he found a skull fracture beneath it and noted that the deceased had an exceptionally thin skull. Although Lewis was found in the river, there was no water in his lungs, indicating that he had not drowned. Davies felt that Lewis had been thrown into the river dead or had accidentally fallen in and died from either exhaustion or his head injury.

Lewis was last seen alive at around midnight on Christmas Eve by his cousin, Thomas Lewis and a friend, William Merchant. At that time, Moses Lewis was bleeding from his head and was so drunk that he was unable to walk. His cousin tried to carry him home on his back but Moses was so intoxicated that, according to Thomas, 'it seemed as if there wasn't a bone in his body,' and he was unable to hold on round his cousin's neck.

Thomas propped Moses against a wall, taking his money from him for safekeeping, then he and Merchant went to try and get a cab. In the early hours of Christmas morning, there were none to be had and Moses eventually told his cousin to go home, saying that he would follow shortly.

Although nobody had actually seen anything amiss, Elizabeth Ann Mitchell told the inquest that a group of men were arguing near where Moses was found and she had distinctly heard one of them say, 'Now, Moses, you bastard, speak the truth.' Thomas Lewis and William Merchant claimed that, when they first came upon Moses, he was having 'cross words' in Welsh with a man named Henry Williams, who admitted to speaking to Moses but denied any argument between them.

In the absence of any concrete evidence, coroner Mr R.J. Rhys suggested that the jury return an open verdict, that the deceased was found dead in the River Taff but that there was nothing to show how he got there.

Cwmaman

David Davies was employed as a stoker at Fforchneol Colliery at Cwmaman near Aberdare, South Wales. On Christmas morning 1880, Richards wanted to go down into the pit to start work but was unable to locate Jonah Thomas, the engineman who was responsible for raising and lowering the miners in cages.

Davies went to the house of over man David Richards, where he found the engineer drinking brandy. Richards gave Davies a tot before the three men went to the pit head together.

Thomas, who was described as 'half drunk', set the engine in motion but instead of the cage descending into the mine, it moved swiftly upwards, dashing so violently against the winding gear that a piece of one of the wheels broke off. Thomas righted the cage and Richards and Davies stepped in, a third man rather wisely declining to join them. Thomas sent the cage down into the mine at a breakneck speed, and during its perilous descent, it collided heavily with the ascending cage.

Davies was hanging on for grim death but Richards was jolted out of the descending cage and, moments after it reached the bottom, his body hit the roof with a terrible thud. (It was suspected that, having been dislodged from the descending cage, he managed to grab onto the ascending one but was unable to maintain his grasp.)

An inquest presided over by coroner Thomas Williams held Jonah Thomas responsible for the death of David Richards and returned a verdict of manslaughter against him. He appeared at the Cardiff Assizes in February 1881, where, having heard evidence that Richards was drinking, the judge decided that he had contributed heavily towards his own death and discharged Thomas, reminding him to keep away from drink in the future as it was 'the curse of the land.'

Holyhead

On Christmas Day 1900, the barque *Primrose Hill* left Liverpool, bound for Vancouver. When she reached the Welsh coast near South Stack, three days later, she fell victim to strong winds and was smashed to pieces.

The steam lifeboat *Duke of Northumberland* made three attempts to reach the stricken ship but was defeated by the mountainous seas. Within sight of land, all but one of the thirty-four man crew perished and those bodies that were recovered after the disaster were almost completely naked, their clothes ripped from them by the sea. Ten of the deceased were apprentices, six of whom were making their very first voyage. The sole survivor, Able Seaman John Ditterson, climbed onto the ship's poop deck and launched himself onto a large wave, which

carried him onto the rocks, from where he was pulled to safety.

In a letter written before he left port, Captain Wilson wrote of the difficulties he had encountered in recruiting a crew, which had delayed the ship's sailing by a week. Had it sailed on time, it would have avoided the storm.

Part of the *Primrose Hill's* cargo was cases of wines and spirits and it was said that the New Year celebrations for many people in the area were enlivened by contraband found on the shore. However, the majority of Holyhead residents were extremely touched by the tragedy and organised a subscription to erect a monument to the deceased, which still stands in the town's Maeshyfryd Cemetery.

Crickhowell

Under cover of darkness during the night of 12/13 July 1869, some person or persons unknown attacked a flock of eighteen young turkeys owned by a farmer at Crickhowell. Using a knife or similar instrument, one leg was amputated from every bird.

All of the birds survived the savagery and it was reported in the contemporary newspapers that the farmer intended to fit each one with a custom-made wooden leg, so that they could continue to be fattened for the lucrative Christmas market.

New Tredegar

Descending to the coalface at New Tredegar, Monmouthshire, on 29 December 1898, for the first time since the Christmas holidays, Henry Saunders fell over in the cage. His body hung partially inside and partially outside and, at great risk to themselves, the other men hung onto his legs and tried to pull him back, while shouting loudly for the cage to be stopped.

The cage was about 300 yards from the bottom and, as it swung from side to side, Saunders was battered against the walls of the shaft. Eventually, his colleagues could no longer hold him and were forced to let him drop.

He fell to his death at the bottom of the shaft, where he was found with one leg severed and his head smashed to a pulp. What caused him to fall was a mystery, although he was known to suffer from occasional fainting fits and it was thought possible that he might have just blacked out. Saunders was twenty-three years old and left a wife and three young children.

Rhoscolyn

At half-past two in the morning of Christmas Day 1891, Edward Jones's daughter Jane woke him to say that she could hear funny noises. As soon as Jones woke, he could smell burning and he quickly traced the source of the smell to the kitchen of the family farm at Rhoscolyn, near Holyhead, where a beam within the chimney had caught fire.

Edward roused his family, including his two brothers, Henry and Owen. He watched both men get out of bed then, thinking that they were following him, he made his way out of the house to safety. Once outside, Edward realised that only Owen was with him and that Henry was still in the burning house.

Together, Edward and Owen circled the house, eventually smashing a window at the back to try and get to Henry. Both men shouted as loudly as they possibly could to try and get their brother to come to the window but without success. When the flames died down, Henry's body was found charred beyond all recognition in the kitchen.

At an inquest held by deputy coroner Dr R. Williams, the jury were told that, on the night of the fire, Henry was the last member of the family to go to bed. Having spent half an hour at the local pub with friends, he was said to be perfectly sober when he left and he went straight to bed when he arrived home at just after eleven o'clock, without needing to use a candle to light his way. Nobody could work out how he failed to escape the blaze and therefore the inquest jury decided that their verdict could only be one of 'accidental death'.

Cyfarthfa

For those without homes, the coke ovens at the Cyfarthfa Iron and Steel Works near Merthyr Tydfil provided a place to sleep on a cold night. Workers there were used to people sneaking in for warmth and shelter and usually ignored the vagrants, since it was not unknown for them to attack those who tried to turn them out.

On 27 December 1900, two men were found dead at the coke ovens, both named Thomas Williams, although they were not related. One had been roasted to death, his body in parts reduced to ashes, while the other was suffocated by fumes.

The police needed to find somewhere to keep the deceased while they awaited the attentions of the coroner. The two bodies were taken to several public houses but were turned away by the landlords, who were unwilling to store the bodies in their out-buildings. The Workhouse refused to admit the bodies to their mortuary, which they maintained was only for those who died at the institution.

The corpses were moved in broad daylight, in full view of anyone who happened to be in the area, and soon a crowd gathered and began to follow the cart bearing the men's bodies. Eventually, a local publican was persuaded to remove his horses from his stable to allow the bodies to be placed there temporarily, and the police gave instructions to the relieving officer to have coffins made. However, they then received a message from the father of one of the victims to say that he would not allow his son's remains to be taken to his home, since he had been a bad boy and his father was not prepared to forgive him.

The police wasted considerable time trying to find somewhere to put the bodies and were eventually granted permission to place them in an outhouse near the Brecon Road Fever Hospital. As soon as darkness fell, the bodies were loaded onto a cart and taken from the pub to their new location.

An inquest was held at Merthyr Police Court by coroner Mr R.J. Rhys, at which the jury returned verdicts of 'accidental death'

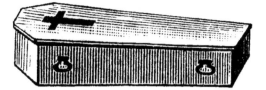

on both men, suggesting that the coke ovens should be fenced. 'Nobody knows the mischief and immorality that goes on there,' agreed the coroner, who then went on to decry the scandal of Merthyr Tydfil having no public mortuary.

Shire Newton

On Christmas Eve 1868, the Shire Newton Brass Band was playing a selection of Christmas carols when famer William Yells took exception to them playing outside his house on the grounds that his children were asleep. He ordered the band to go away but bandsman William Bryant told them to play on.

Angrily, Yells kicked the band's drum, although he didn't damage it. He then took William by the collar and propelled him well away from his house. Bandsman Charles Bryant tried to defend his brother but he too was picked up by the collar and frogmarched off. The two brothers were most unhappy about being manhandled and combined forces against Yells, who received a black eye and a badly cut hand, which he claimed was done by a knife.

The upshot of the affray was that both Bryant brothers found themselves before magistrates at Chepstow Police Court on 28 December charged with assaulting Yells.

The defence was that Yells started the tussle by kicking the drum and then turning on the two defendants. The prosecution contended that, in common with the rest of the band, the Bryant brothers were drunk and, in refusing to desist from playing when asked, had provoked Yells to react as he did.

Although there was no evidence that either of the brothers was in possession of a knife, magistrates sentenced each brother to six weeks' imprisonment with hard labour.

Markham

On Christmas Eve 1938, Emily Gwynneth Weed of Markham in Monmouthshire was left to keep the excited children entertained. It was a task that the fifteen-year-old girl relished and she threw herself into telling them a Christmas story.

The children listened in wonder as Emily pretended to speak to Father Christmas by calling up the chimney. Unfortunately, as she did so, her dress caught fire. The children's screams alerted next-door neighbour Daisy Frost and she rushed into Emily's house and wrapped her in a mat to extinguish the flames, before arranging for a neighbour with a car to take her to the doctor.

Sadly, Emily died in hospital and almost her last words were to remind her father to fill the children's stockings.

Cardiff

On 27 December 1891, William Smith, a nightshift worker at Anthony's Brewery, returned to his home on Union Street, Cardiff at 6.30 a.m. and, on opening the front door, found his house full of smoke. He roused his next-door neighbour, Thomas Griffiths, and sent him for help before breaking into the back of the house.

By that time, much of the smoke had cleared and when Griffiths arrived with PC Green, the men were able to see that a sofa and chairs in the kitchen and part of the staircase were on fire. Tragically, Smith's twenty-eight-year-old wife, Elizabeth, lay on the kitchen floor, her body burned so badly that parts of it crumbled to ash when touched.

PC Green was able to extinguish the fire with a couple of buckets of water, enabling the men to get upstairs to where three-year-old William junior lay in his bed, as if sleeping. He had been suffocated by the smoke and although PC Green made desperate efforts to revive him, he was beyond help.

Elizabeth was in the habit of rising early every morning to light the fire and put the kettle on, so that her husband had a hot drink to greet him when he arrived home from work. The remains of a paraffin lamp were found on the stairs and the coroner theorised that Mrs Smith had either tripped or spilled the oil as she went downstairs, setting light to her clothing. (Although her body was badly burned, a post-mortem examination revealed that she had died from suffocation.)

The inquest jury returned verdicts of 'accidental death' on both mother and son.

Newport

One of the ancient customs associated with Christmas in Wales is the Mari Lwyd, which translates literally as the grey mare. The Mari Lwyd comprised a horse's skull, or a replica of one, mounted on a pole, to which false ears and eyes were attached and reins and bells added. It was then carried door-to-door by a party of people, hoping to be admitted to the house for food and drink. The Mari party sang traditional Welsh songs and recited improvised verses, to which the occupants of the house were supposed to reply in kind until, eventually, the battle of verse was won or lost when one of the parties ran out of words.

At Christmas 1834, a group of ten men assembled in a tenement to make a Mari Lwyd. They intended to decorate it with tar, which they heated on the fire, but, before too long, it boiled over and began to burn furiously.

One of the men snatched the tar from the fire and tried to throw it outside, not realising that the door was closed. The boiling liquid scattered round the room, burning everyone it came into contact with and starting a fire. One of the men thought to open a window and climb through, at which all of them fled, some jumping into water, others ripping off their burning clothes as they ran.

Only one man stayed behind, to try and save his child from the inferno. Sadly, he was unsuccessful and the little boy was burned to a cinder.

Swansea

On Christmas Eve 1884, a devastating fire broke out at the premises of pawnbroker Mr Goldstone at Swansea, trapping the occupants in the burning building. Mr and Mrs Goldstone and

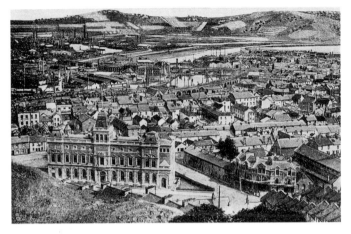

Bird's eye view of Swansea. (Author's collection)

their servant were rescued using a portable fire escape, which was permanently located about 30 yards away. Even though Mr Goldstone's assistant, Philip Freeman, knew of the existence of the fire escape, he chose to jump from an upper storey window rather than wait for it to be brought the short distance to the shop. He fell more than 40 feet and died almost instantly on landing.

The premises and all of the stock were completely destroyed.

Pen-y-Graig, Rhondda Valley

Seventy-five-year-old Henry Morgan and his sixty-nine-year-old wife, Mary, were both heavy drinkers and, on Christmas Eve 1900, the barman at their local public house in Pen-y-Graig refused to serve them because they were drunk. That evening, Henry, who was partially crippled, went to another pub, where he bought two bottles of beer and a bottle of rum to take out.

Later, the couple were heard having what was described as 'a deuce of a row', during which Henry swore in Welsh and English and threatened to kill his wife. A few minutes later, he went to a neighbour and said, 'The poor old woman is dead.'

Mary was indeed dead. She was bruised black and blue all over her body and had two broken ribs, which had punctured a lung.

She was also malnourished and had an enlarged
liver due to drinking. A post-mortem examination showed that the cause of death was a
combination of shock and a large blood clot on
Mary's brain, which the doctor suggested resulted from being
beaten with a weapon such as a crutch or walking stick, both
of which Henry used to walk.

At the inquest on Mary's death, Henry asked if he might
say something and, granted permission, he sobbed, 'I never
put my hand upon her poor body . . . Neither the weight of
my fist or crutches or walking stick was on her . . . I never
touched my poor old sweetheart.'

The inquest jury believed that Mary's injuries were caused
by her husband but, since they did not think that the killing was premeditated, they returned a verdict of manslaughter
rather than murder against Henry Morgan. The jury at his
trial at the Assizes in Cardiff on 22 March 1901 concurred and,
even though he was indicted for wilful murder, they found
him guilty of the lesser offence of manslaughter. He was sentenced to five years' penal servitude.

SCOTLAND

Glasgow

On Christmas Eve 1927, fire broke out in a multi-storey building containing business premises, warehouses and workshops in Graham Square, Glasgow, a *cul de sac* off the Gallowgate. The fire was discovered at just after eight o'clock in the evening and within ten minutes of the alarm being raised, there was an explosion and the north end of the building crashed to the ground.

Fire engines were summoned from every fire station in the area to try and prevent the blaze from spreading to adjoining tenements, where more than fifty families resided, and at one time there were more than sixty firemen at work. It took two hours before the area was considered safe enough for the residents to return to their smoke- and water-damaged homes.

It was decided to leave a small crew of firemen on the scene damping down and at that point, a roll call was carried out and four firemen were found to be missing. Their colleagues spent two days carefully picking through tons of debris at the hazardous site trying to find their bodies, which were eventually found in a corner of a warehouse. Henry McKellar (40) and James Conn (31) were both married men, Conn having three children. David Jeffrey (24) supported his widowed mother and Morrison Dunbar (23) had only four months' service with the Fire Brigade. Tragically, when the alarm was raised, all of the men were taking part in a Christmas party with their families at the fire station.

Elliott Junction, near Arbroath

The Scotch Express train left King's Cross on 27 December 1906 and got as far as Arbroath before it could go no further. The line ahead was blocked with heavy snow and the express train waited at Arbroath Station for several hours, before it was decided to make up a small train to return the passengers to either Edinburgh or Dundee.

Before setting off, driver George Gourlay was given strict instructions to go very cautiously, to stop at all the stations, and to keep a very good look out for the local train ahead of him. However, when Gourlay's train met the local train at Elliott Junction about two miles from Arbroath, it ploughed straight into it.

Twenty-two people were killed including Alexander William Black, the Member of Parliament for Banffshire, and stoker Robert Irvine, who was pinned beneath his overturned engine for seven hours before being released and taken to Arbroath Infirmary, where he died hours later.

The weather conditions at the time of the crash were appalling, described by one survivor as 'a boiling mass of snow'. Gourlay maintained that he never even saw the local train until he crashed into it and that, until then, all the signals were clear. However, when Gourlay was examined by a doctor in the immediate aftermath of the crash, he was said to be drunk and, as a result, he was arrested and charged with culpable homicide.

He was tried at the Edinburgh Assizes but, in a trial lasting several days, there was a great deal of conflicting evidence. Gourlay insisted that his speed at the time of the crash was below twenty miles per hour but some witnesses believed that he was travelling much faster.

It was known that someone had given sixty-year-old Gourlay a glass of brandy for shock immediately after the crash, although the doctor who pronounced him drunk believed that this was insufficient alcohol to have affected him so badly. In addition, it was alleged that Gourlay had been drinking whisky in the station snack bar before setting off on his fateful journey and it was argued that his head injury, shock and even the intense cold could have contributed to his appearance of intoxication.

Gourlay had worked for the North British Railway Company for forty-seven years and, prior to the crash, his record had been unblemished and exemplary. By a majority, the trial jury found him guilty of culpable homicide, although they believed that there were extenuating circumstances and thus Gourlay was sentenced to just five months' imprisonment.

Glasgow

On Christmas Day 1909, a football match took place between Partick Thistle and Hibernian at Firhill Stadium, Glasgow. The stadium had only been open for three months and at an inspection prior to the start of the match, the pitch was said to be treacherously icy. 'You are risking life and limb asking anyone to play out there,' one of the Hibernian players is said to have commented, but, since thousands of fans had already assembled to see the game, it was decided that the match would go on.

It was proving to be a bad day for Hibernian, whose captain felt unwell on the train to the match and declared himself unfit to play. Then, in the pre-match warm up, the vice-captain hurt his knee and was forced to withdraw. Twenty-three-year-old James Main was appointed captain in their absence and Hibs managed to open the scoring. However, as half-time approached, Main was injured in a sliding tackle and was obviously unfit to continue playing. He was helped to the changing rooms and took no further part in the match, which Partick won by three goals to one.

Main was fit enough to drink tea with his team mates and to travel home by train, walking the last half mile from the station. However, later that night he became unwell and a doctor was called. With the imprint of the opposing player's boot clearly visible on Main's chest, the doctor diagnosed severe bruising but Main collapsed and was rushed to Edinburgh hospital, where a perforated bowel was diagnosed. Although Main was operated on, he died from his injuries on 29 December 1909.

The player who tackled him, Frank Branscombe, had slipped on the icy field and his foot accidentally caught Main as he fell.

Note: Some sources give the cause of Main's death as a perforated spleen.

Rutherglen, near Glasgow ❦❦❦

Farmer John Mason was plagued by potato thieves and, towards Christmas 1842, his store was plundered several times during the night. Mason gave his seventeen-year-old servant John McBryde a loaded gun and put him on watch. However, the potato thief or thieves were clever and twice waited until McBryde took a break to warm himself in the house before raiding the potato bin.

The night of 23 December was bitterly cold and stormy and once again McBryde left his post to go and get warm. However, when he returned, he caught three potato thieves red-handed. He fired his gun and the men abandoned their half-filled sacks and fled.

It never occurred to either McBryde or John Mason that the shot may have hit anybody until the following morning, when a dead body was found less than 50 yards from the potato bin. The man was identified as John (or James) Allan, a former quarryman.

Allan had lost one arm and the sight of one eye in a work accident, after which he was forced to give up quarrying. He took a job as a nightwatchman but lost it after a bout of fever and was then unable to obtain work and was forced to keep himself, his wife and four children on 3s 6d a week earned by a grown-up daughter, supplemented with 1s, as well as 8lbs of oatmeal, provided from the poor funds.

McBryde was charged with both murder and culpable murder, appearing at the Circuit Court in Glasgow, where he pleaded guilty to the charge of culpable homicide with no intent to maim, sobbing as he did so. Having heard several character witnesses, who testified that McBryde was mild and inoffensive, the judges were unable to decide on an appropriate sentence and forwarded the case to the High Court of Judiciary in Edinburgh.

The Court sat on 10 June 1843 and after hearing all the evidence, Lord Meadowbank addressed McBryde, saying that, taking into account all the circumstances of the case in conjunction with the defendant's youth and previously excellent character, and the fact that his master had placed a loaded gun into his hands, the Court did not feel that severe punishment was necessary.

Although allowed bail after the offence, McBryde was sent to Glasgow Prison after his trial and the High Court sentenced him to serve one additional month's imprisonment.

Coatbridge

The Phoenix Iron Works in Coatbridge had been closed for the Christmas period since Christmas Eve 1892 but early on the morning of 27 December, a team of fifteen men were brought in to get up steam ready for the resumption of work.

At about three o'clock in the morning, there was a massive explosion, which sent a great shower of bricks, stones and other debris across the main street. Much of it fell into the Clifton Iron Works, which stood opposite the Phoenix, and three men working there were injured. One of the five boilers was carried more than 50 yards, demolishing the engine shop when it fell. The Phoenix Works were situated on the main street of Coatbridge and the windows of every house for hundreds of yards in every direction were smashed by the blast.

When a search was made of what remained of the boiler room at Phoenix, the mutilated bodies of two boiler firemen, George Telford and James Watt, were found in the wreckage. It was thought that frozen pipes were the main cause of the explosion and a Board of Trade inquiry concurred. However, they found the proprietor of the works negligent for not providing overnight supervision for the boilers and fined him £20. The boiler feeder was also fined £5 for carelessness.

Note: Some contemporary newspapers name James Watt as James Brewsterford.

Flannan Islands

The Flannan Islands are a small group of islands in the Outer Hebrides, the largest of which is Islean Mòr, where a lighthouse was constructed between 1895 and 1899.

On Boxing Day 1900, *Hesperus* sailed out to the lighthouse with supplies and a relief keeper. (The trip should have happened on 20 December but was delayed due to bad weather.) It was almost immediately evident that something was amiss, as there was no sign of keepers Thomas Marshall, James Ducat and Donald Macarthur.

Jim Harvie, the captain of *Hesperus*, blew his whistle and fired off a distress flare but neither elicited any response from the lighthouse. Eventually relief keeper Joseph Moore was put ashore and found the island deserted. The entrance gate to the compound and the lighthouse door were both closed, the beds unmade and the clocks stopped. The only sign of anything remotely untoward was an overturned chair in the kitchen. One set of oilskins left behind showed that one of the keepers had left the building in his shirt sleeves.

Leaving Moore and three volunteers to man the lighthouse, Harvie sailed back to shore, where he despatched a telegram to the Northern Lighthouse Board. Meanwhile, those left at the lighthouse began a search for clues.

The log was made up until 9 a.m. on 15 December but a ship's captain had already reported passing the lighthouse at about midnight on that date and not seeing the light. There was every indication that the men disappeared during the afternoon of 15 December and there was evidence of bad weather at the time.

On 29 December, a representative of the Northern Lighthouse Board arrived to conduct an official inquiry. Robert Muirhead's report concluded that the men were on duty up till dinner time on 15 December, when, in bad weather, they went to secure a box in which the mooring ropes, landing ropes and other equipment were kept, which was located in a crevice in the rock about 110 feet above sea level. An extra-large wave rushed up the face of the rock and swept them completely away. Muirhead's report doesn't explain why Donald Macarthur left the lighthouse in a storm in his shirt sleeves, especially since, in doing so, he would have been in breach of NLB rules by leaving the light unattended.

No bodies were ever found and the mystery remains unsolved. Various theories have been advanced over the years, ranging from suggestions that one of the keepers went insane and murdered the others before committing suicide, to more esoteric explanations, such as alien abduction.

Musselburgh

On Christmas Day 1884, twenty-seven-year-old Christina Smith of Musselburgh, near Edinburgh, cut the throat of her nine-month-old daughter, Annie Reston Smith, then cut her own. Christina's husband, William, had gone to help a neighbour with a little job and returned home at ten o'clock in the evening to find his wife and baby dead in a pool of blood on the kitchen floor, an open razor lying nearby.

Thankfully, the couple's other two children were sleeping peacefully and it seemed as though their mother had put them to bed before ending her own life and that of her baby. The Smith's neighbours had heard nothing untoward and it was thought that Christina and Annie would both have died almost instantly due to blood loss from their horrific wounds.

Although Christina was described as having been 'in depressed spirits', nobody had ever imagined that she posed the slightest risk to herself or the children. An inquest later determined that Christina had killed Annie and committed suicide while of unsound mind.

Paisley

Quarryman Patrick Brogan was working at the Enderslie Quarry in Paisley on Christmas Eve 1894, when he met with a terrible accident. As he was ramming home a charge of gelignite into a hole in order to blast the rock, the gelignite suddenly exploded, blowing the wooden rod that he was using for tamping clear through his body. The rod entered his chest and exited beneath his shoulder blade, projecting 3 feet from his back.

The rod had to be cut down in order to fit Brogan into an ambulance and although he was taken to hospital, he died on Christmas Day, leaving a wife and children. An inquest later recorded a verdict of 'accidental death'.

Stotfield

On Christmas Day 1806, the weather at Stotfield dawned fair and the town's three fishing boats went out onto calm seas. They were

Stotfield from the beach, Lossiemouth. (Author's collection)

fishing only a mile or two from the shore but, as the morning progressed, a fierce gale came in from the south-west and by eleven o'clock it was described as having the appearance and force of a tornado. The three fishing boats were swept away from the shore and eventually went down with all hands. In total, twenty-one men died, leaving seventeen widows and forty-two children to mourn their loss and making Stotfield a village from which practically all the menfolk had been eliminated at a stroke.

Dundee

On Christmas Eve 1912, a fire broke out in a jute warehouse in Dundee, causing around £10,000 worth of damage. Firemen spent most of the day tackling the blaze and, as evening approached, were confident that it was under control.

However, the jute within the warehouse was affected by the heat and water and began to swell, pushing one of the warehouse walls outwards. The wall toppled onto a small house occupied by stable hand George Low and his family.

Mrs Low had just put her four children to bed and filled their stockings with Christmas presents when the wall crushed the house. The firemen were already on the scene and quickly began to dig through the rubble, rescuing Mrs Low, who suffered only minor injuries. However, there was no sign of the four children, aged between eight months and eight years old, who all perished. Eight horses in an adjoining stable were also killed.

Tay Bridge, Dundee

On 28 December 1879, Scotland was hit by a terrible storm with winds gusting to gale force eleven. As a train was crossing the bridge between Wormit and Dundee, the structure suddenly collapsed, plunging the engine, six carriages and all of the passengers and crew into the Firth of Tay.

There were no survivors and it was estimated that seventy-five people died, although that figure was only arrived at by examining ticket sales from stations as far afield as London. Although divers and a flotilla of small boats patrolled the Firth for many days after the tragedy, only forty-six bodies were ever recovered, the last of which was not pulled from the water until February 1880.

As the bodies were recovered, newspapers published their identities and snippets of information about their lives. Robert Watson's wife was so distraught at hearing of the death of her husband and two eldest sons that she completely lost her reason and was admitted to a lunatic asylum, effectively leaving the couple's two youngest children without a father or mother.

The engine from the Tay Bridge disaster. (Author's collection)

The old Tay Bridge after the disaster. (Author's collection)

James Crighton was travelling home after attending his father's funeral on 22 December, thus his elderly mother lost her husband and son within a week.

The bridge was, at the time, the longest in the world, at over two miles in length and had been open for less than two years. An inquiry into the disaster found that the construction of the bridge was inadequate, being unable to stand the force of the high winds and the weight of the train. The bridge was eventually much strengthened and reopened and the train was recovered and, after repairs, put back into service.

Fort William

Although it was the festive season, work continued without a break on the Lochaber Water Power Scheme.

On Christmas Day 1931, a team of men were involved in the construction of the proposed tunnel linking Loch Trieg and Loch Laggan when there was a sudden explosion, which blew men in all directions. Dennis J. Green and Patrick Quigley, who were both from Ireland, died instantly and five of their colleagues were badly injured and were taken to hospital at Fort William by ambulance. All are believed to have survived.

Galston 🌿

On 27 December 1881, a group of boys were in a schoolroom at Glebedykes Public School at Galston, East Ayrshire. They were being supervised by headmaster Mr Burnside but he had to step out of the room for a moment and during his absence twelve-year-old John Bowie borrowed a knife to scratch some figures on his slate.

As he was doing so, thirteen-year-old David Richmond walked by and made a caustic remark to Bowie, at the same time cuffing him lightly on the cheek. As Richmond returned to his seat, Bowie angrily shouted, 'You will catch it later for that.'

Richmond got up and walked towards Bowie, who ran from the room. Richmond followed and was just lifting his foot to kick Bowie when the younger boy rounded on him and threw the knife at him. Richmond ducked and the knife sailed past him, through the open door into the classroom and embedded itself in the chest of twelve-year-old James Adams.

'Oh, the knife is in me!' Adams exclaimed before staggering forwards a few steps and collapsing.

Adams died almost immediately and Bowie was charged with culpable homicide. He appeared at the Kilmarnock Sherriff's Court on 23 January 1882, where he was found guilty and ordered to pay a £10 fine or spend thirty days in prison. His parents paid the fine.

Peterhead 🌿

Over Christmas 1914, parts of Scotland suffered from storms and high winds and by Boxing Day, these had increased almost to hurricane force.

At eleven o'clock in the morning, the Hull trawler *Tom Tit* tried to seek shelter in Peterhead harbour but was washed onto 'The Horseback', a large rock close to the harbour entrance. A large crowd of spectators assembled on the shore and were watching the *Tom Tit's* progress with an ever-increasing sense of doom. Fearing that she was about to be wrecked, James Graneham (or Grantham) attempted to swim out to her with a rope but was beaten back by the waves. A naval officer, Lieutenant Currie, also attempted to swim to the vessel but his rope snapped and he was dashed onto rocks and had to be hauled to safety.

The town's lifeboat *Alexander Tulloch* was launched but, as she reached the harbour entrance, a huge wave washed her westwards onto rocks. Three of the crew jumped clear of the lifeboat and were helped to safety but the remaining nine were swept out of the boat. One was rescued in an injured

condition, having become entangled with something in the boat, which prevented him from being thrown clear. Another was washed into a pool known locally as 'Bobby's Hole' and a man jumped in and briefly managed to grab him, before the lifeboat man was pulled from his grasp by the strength of the sea.

The men from the *Alexander Tulloch* were rapidly floating towards Smith Embankment and those on the shore followed them. Someone jumped in and rescued the coxswain, who had managed to hold onto an oar and thus stayed afloat and a young man named James Imlach went into the water with a rope around his waist and managed to drag another crewman to safety. Two of the crew were wearing lifebelts and one was washed ashore alive. The second was unconscious and, in spite of valiant efforts made by the town's doctors, he died.

Thomas Adams, David Murray Strachan and James Geddes junior lost their lives and their lifeboat was completely destroyed. The crew of the *Tom Tit* were all rescued.

Cowdenbeath

On Christmas Eve 1920, two Cowdenbeath men lost their lives in separate accidents in different pits. At Gordon Pit at Raith Colliery, thirty-eight-year-old shunter Thomas Blyth Forbes was sitting on an empty coal waggon, which was accidentally run into by several loaded waggons. The empty waggon overturned and Forbes was crushed beneath it.

On the same day, twenty-five-year-old George Chapman was killed instantly by a large boulder, which fell from the roof of the coal seam he was working at number 10 Pit, Kirkford Colliery. He left a widow and three children.

Inquests returned verdicts of 'accidental death' on both men.

Edinburgh

On Christmas Day 1885, Mr McInulty of Big Jack's Close, Edinburgh was taking his three-year-old son Neil to visit relatives. They were about to leave the house when McInulty had to return momentarily to leave his wife some money. While his father was otherwise occupied, Neil wandered out of the house by himself and walked across the road.

Sadly, he chose to cross between two carts fully laden with lime and the second one ran him over, the wheel passing over his neck and killing him instantly. Carter Thomas Adams was taken into custody for questioning but released when it was obvious that he bore no responsibility for Neil's tragic death.

Glasgow

Heavy snow in Glasgow on Boxing Day 1925 brought out the area's children in droves and there were two fatal sledging accidents. Ten-year-old James Donald sustained a fractured skull after crashing into a car while on his toboggan, dying from his injuries later that night.

At Queen's Park Recreation Ground, thirteen-year-old Isabella Kerr smashed into a goal post while sledging down a steep hill. She incurred severe internal injuries, which proved fatal within hours. Isabella's toboggan was a Christmas present.

Rutherglen

The disused Westfield Quarry at Rutherglen, Lanarkshire, frequently froze over and, although it was fenced, it proved an irresistible draw to the area's children.

On Boxing Day 1876, a number of children trespassed on the quarry to slide on the ice. At the edges, the ice was very thick and more than capable of bearing weight but further out into the quarry, where the water was up to 30 feet deep, the ice was much more fragile.

John Shields ventured a little too far from the bank and fell through the ice. He was able to swim a little and managed to keep himself afloat. Peter Cassell rushed to try and save him but he too fell into the water and, having only one arm, quickly sank.

The other children ran to find an adult and although there were still air bubbles on the surface of the water when assistance arrived, all that was visible of the boys was their caps, floating in the holes in the ice.

BIBLIOGRAPHY

Aberdeen Journal
Belfast Newsletter
Berrow's Worcester Journal
Bristol Mercury
Bury and Norwich Post and Suffolk Standard
Caledonian Mercury
Daily Mail
Daily News
Daily Sketch
Derby Mercury
Doncaster Chronicle
Dundee Courier
Dunfermline Journal
Essex Standard
Freeman's Journal
Glasgow Herald
Glasgow Journal
Glasgow Saturday Post
Hampshire / Portsmouth Telegraph
Holyhead and Anglesey Mail
Illustrated Police News
Ipswich Journal
Jackson's Oxford Journal
Leeds Intelligence

Leicester Chronicle
Liverpool Mercury
Manchester Guardian
Manchester Times
Morning Chronicle
Morning Post
Newcastle Courant
Newcastle Journal
Newry Telegraph
Northern Echo
North Wales Chronicle
Observer
Plymouth and Cornish Advertiser
Royal Cornwall Gazette
Scotsman
Sussex Weekly Advertiser
Telegraph
The Era
The Standard
The Times
Trewman's Exeter Flying Post
Western Mail
Wigan Observer
Wolverhampton Chronicle
Wrexham Weekly Advertiser

ALSO BY THE AUTHOR